DANCE HIST

DANCE HISTORY

A Methodology for Study

Edited by
JANET ADSHEAD
and
JUNE LAYSON

DANCE BOOKS LTD
9 Cecil Court, London WC2N 4EZ

First published in 1983 by Dance Books Ltd,
9 Cecil Court, London WC2N 4EZ

Reprinted 1986

ISBN 0 903102 74 9

© 1983 Janet Adshead and June Layson

Design and production in association with
Book Production Consultants, 47 Norfolk Street, Cambridge

Printed and bound by The Burlington Press (Cambridge) Limited,
Foxton, Cambridge

ACKNOWLEDGEMENTS

Between 1972 and 1981 approximately fifty students followed courses in dance history as part of a Master's degree at the University of Leeds. The impetus for this text derives directly from the experience of that course and the editors wish to thank all the students who in various ways contributed to the development of dance history studies.

Particular use has been made of the archive of the London Festival Ballet and we are very grateful for the assistance given.

The editors acknowledge with gratitude permission given by the Roehampton Institute to reproduce units of study in dance history.

NOTES ON THE AUTHORS

Janet Adshead, Cert.Ed. Adv.Dip.Ed. M.A.(Dist.) Ph.D.
Leverhulme Research Fellow in Dance, University of Surrey. Formerly Senior Lecturer, Dartford College of Education (Thames Polytechnic); Research Fellow in Dance, University of Leeds; first award by S.S.R.C. for doctoral research in dance. Member of C.N.A.A. Dance Board.

Theresa Buckland, B.A.(Hons.)
Lecturer in dance at Bretton Hall College of Higher Education; organiser of first two conferences in the U.K. on 'Traditional Dance'; doctoral student in Folk Life Studies, University of Leeds.

Judith A. Chapman, Cert.Ed. Dip.P.E. M.A.
Research Officer, National Resource Centre for Dance of the University of Surrey; formerly Senior Lecturer in dance at Bedford College of Higher Education; doctoral research on resource centres for dance, University of Surrey.

Michael Huxley, B.Ed.(Hons.) M.A.
Part-time lecturer in dance history at Leicester Polytechnic; doctoral research in Early European modern dance, University of Leeds.

June Layson, Cert.Ed. D.A.S.E. M.Ed.
Director of Dance Studies, University of Surrey and Director of the National Resource Centre for Dance. Developed Master's degree courses in dance at the University of Leeds from 1971–81. Member of the Gulbenkian Foundation enquiry into Dance Education and Training, member of the Arts Council's dance and regional advisory panels and C.N.A.A. Dance Board. Doctoral research, Isadora Duncan.

Patricia A. Mitchinson, Dip.L.C.D.D. B.Ed.(Hons.) M.A.
Lecturer and Principal of the Harrogate School of Dance and Drama. Teacher of R.A.D./I.S.T.D. and G.C.E. 'O' level Ballet.

Joan W. White, Cert.Ed. Dip.P.E. B.A. M.A.
Senior Lecturer in Dance, Roehampton Institute, London. Moderator for the University of London G.C.E. 'O', 'A' and 16+ exams.

CONTENTS

Introduction

In preparing this text the editors have had in mind the increasing interest in the history of dance both among the general dance public and, more particularly, in universities, polytechnics, colleges and schools where dance is a subject of study. With the growth in dance scholarship has come the realisation that methods employed in the past have often been implicit rather than overtly stated and that broadly based accounts of dance which cover long time spans have resulted in sweeping statements about the nature of dance and its function in society. In relation to the first point, there has been no fully worked out theoretical basis for dance history as distinct from other types of history. While a historical study of dance will share basic concerns with a history of any form of human activity, the fact that it is *dance* determines the nature and form of the enquiry. In relation to the second point, the resulting texts have been less reliable in description and less accurate in interpretation of the dance than would now be the case following recent improvements in methodology.

The American Committee on Research in Dance, in the proceedings of its second conference held in 1969 (*CORD* 1970), remarked on the lack of dance research methodologies that the first conference had identified, and contended that

> the findings from carefully designed historical research could be beneficial in establishing a perspective from which to view the disparate and essential cultural and educational roles of dance in America.
>
> (*CORD* 1970, p.vii)

The second conference brought together studies of various types and subsequent publications have begun to develop a historical methodology. These publications are specialist research documents which are not easily available in the U.K. (details may be found in Appendix A).

One of the differences in approach between the American initiative and the present one is that in the U.S. they chose deliberately to start from disciplines other than dance, from history, anthropology, drama and other arts, while we chose to start from the dance. Perhaps we shall meet on the way. Certainly they have already

1

found that the area of reconstruction requires 'dance' scholarship and not solely historical study.

What there is to study as 'dance history' and *how* it might be approached are the two central concerns of the editors.

June Layson's experience at Leeds University between 1970 and 1980 of mounting the first Master's degree level history of dance course in the United Kingdom has been the motivation for the text. At the present time dance history is often inadequately taught at the undergraduate level and is almost non-existent in schools despite the general recognition of its value. There seemed therefore to be a need for a text which would provide a reasoned argument for the place of dance history, a detailed methodology of procedures which can be followed and a number of examples of these methods in practice. The examples were chosen to take account of two major characteristics of dance history; firstly, that it is based on many different kinds of evidence or source material and secondly, that the form of dance being studied may be one of many types. Dance is not uniform and the evidence of its existence may come from a multitude of sources.

The present text focuses on dance in the Western world and particularly on dance in the U.K. While the structural basis proposed in Part I for the study of dance history applies to the history of all dance forms and cultures, the selection of examples in Parts II and III reflects current knowledge, the availability of primary source material and the pressing need to examine our British dance heritage.

In relation to teaching dance history, some of the possibilities for constructing courses are explored and the requirements of writing dance history are examined.

The Appendices include a bibliography of sources and information about the newly formed National Resource Centre for Dance of the University of Surrey.

Janet Adshead and June Layson
March 1983

Reference

CORD 1970 'Dance history research: perspectives from related arts and disciplines' ed: Kealiinohomoku, J. *Proceedings of the Second Conference on research in dance*

PART I

A rationale and methodology for dance history

The three chapters which together constitute Part I contain an examination of different but related aspects of a possible theoretical framework for the study of dance history. In the first chapter the stress is on the importance and relevance of a historical perspective for an understanding of dance in the widest sense of the very many manifestations that exist all over the world in the present time and that have existed in the past. A model is proposed which focuses attention on the dance, first and foremost, and locates it on a time continuum. The geographical location of the dance is a further significant factor.

In addition, the place of historical study of dance within the educational system is analysed since it is in this context that such study most usually takes place.

In Chapter 2 the various materials that are the basis of dance history and some of the ways of setting about such study are discussed. The different processes that are used and the particular skills that have to be acquired are described. This is followed by a brief consideration of some of the outcomes of the study of dance history and a characterisation of what counts as good historical communication.

Examples of good historical studies of dance form the basis of Chapter 3. A number of texts which are widely available are described, summarised and evaluated for their usefulness in particular types of dance history. This chapter is intended as an examination of the nature and value of some central texts as examples of historical writing. The process of critical analysis is demonstrated and the use of the texts described.

3

CHAPTER 1

The historical perspective in the study of dance

by Janet Adshead

1.1 The historical perspective
1.2 Dance within the historical perspective
1.3 Choreography, performance and appreciation
1.4 Genre, style and structure
1.5 The place of the historical study of dance in education
1.6 Learning processes in the study of dance history

1.1 *The historical perspective*
The relevance of a historical perspective for the understanding of any human activity is often questioned. Direct participation in the activity itself, in this case in dancing and in making dances, is seen by many people to be of paramount value. Indeed, unless people dance, there would be nothing to have a history of. However, this is to minimise the importance of a historical understanding and to fail to see its potential to enrich knowledge in and of dance. Understanding of dance can develop in a number of ways but to ignore the historical and contextual factors which explain and give rise to the existence of any one particular form or type of dance is to run the risk of misunderstanding its function.

The basic concern of historical study is to pinpoint change through time and to study important events. It requires not merely a chronicle but an explanation of events and an unravelling of the interconnections between them. In human terms it seems necessary to have the sense of identity and continuity that comes from an understanding of history, and this applies in all areas of human endeavour. In relation to dance it may be possible, in consequence of historical study, to understand why the many different kinds of dance have evolved in the way they have. Historical study is a search, not just for facts, but for reasons to explain developments in the interests of acquiring a deeper understanding of dance. Looking

4

at dance through the time perspective allows a long-term 'objective' view of its changing forms.

Whether a truly 'objective' account can ever be possible, either written by contemporary or later writers, or historians, is much debated. Clearly any individual is a product of the age in which she/he lives and will therefore view an event from that background; but this does not mean that reasoned argument on historical matters is impossible.

However, on its own, a purely chronological approach, which considers dance events through time, is not sufficient since the particular era in which a dance exists has a complete *cultural setting*. It is only in the light of an understanding of the social significance of a particular dance that meaningful study can take place. The focus on a moment in time in conjunction with cultural understanding guides attention to those contextual factors which are *relevant* to the study of that dance within that distinctive historical setting.

In this sense the purpose of the dance (i.e. its function) can be seen to be derived from its context. As a result, historical study can be more closely defined, for example, as that of dance as art, as ritual, as a social or educative force. To ignore the cultural perspective on dance encourages superficial accounts of its function.

In a further and quite different way the dance may have social relevance. For example, protagonists both of classical and modern ballet as well as modern dance might claim that the themes the dances portray are immediately relevant to society. Despite this, the actual movements used in the dance may date back two hundred years if they are from the classical ballet repertoire. So, in this instance, a historical appreciation would be vital to an understanding of the dance.

The *geographical location* of dance styles is an important variable. Not only does dance vary through time, it also varies across the world. Its physical situation in Africa or Asia or Europe substantially affects its nature. The dance then acquires a '*place*' perspective and when this is added to the time perspective it produces a model of dance studies through time and with regard to its place.

It may be in part the result of geographical location that each society, each race, nation and continent is distinctive in culture. Dance forms reflect and are part of a cultural framework. The dance may function within that frame in different ways at different times, and specific forms of dance may have several functions at the same

5

moment in time in relation to that society. If the dance functions as an art, or as an act of worship, or as a means of social interaction then an accurate description in detail is dependent upon a clear notion of that function. The relation of any one dance to its culture is exceedingly complex. The theoretical background which leads to understanding of why dances function as they do, comes from a different set of constructs in each case – for example, from anthropology, from ritual/religious studies, or from art theory and aesthetics. Anthropological and sociological studies are only just beginning to yield a picture of dance in its full cultural diversity. It would be facile to expect to state briefly the subtle and varied purposes of dance.

1.2 *Dance within the historical perspective*

A model for the history of dance which begins from the premise that the dance is the centre of attention must start from those concerns which characterise dance and distinguish it from any other activity and which, in consequence, require distinctive study processes. The problems, interests and issues involved in the study of dance cohere around the *making*, *performing* and *appreciation* of dance as a structured form of human movement. It may be structured in order to have a magical, social or artistic significance, but the dance is still recognisable as 'dance' in all these contexts.

In order that there should be no confusion or misunderstanding it should be emphasised that these characterisations apply not only to dance as an art in this century in the Western world, but to any and all manifestations of dance, in any society, and at any time. Attempts at exclusive definitions of forms of dance fail dismally in the face of the complexity and overlapping character of many forms. *Characterisation* of different kinds of dance is not thereby denied, it is instead seen to reveal the richness and multiplicity of facets of the dance.

An important distinction must be made between the dance structure itself (its formal arrangement of elements), the process of making the dance, and the people who make and perform it since different factors come into play in considering each aspect. The terms 'choreography' and 'performance', which are commonly used, tend to encompass both the made form (the dance) and the making process, and therefore to obscure statements of what is being

6

discussed. The following sections characterise the concepts of choreography, performance and appreciation, both generally and specifically, within a historical perspective.

1.3 *Choreography, performance and appreciation*

The conceptual structure of choreography, performance and appreciation described here underpins this book, and these notions, as well as the artefacts which result, i.e. the dances, can be seen as being historically variable. Isolating *changes* in dance forms, in techniques and steps, in the manner of performance, etc., locating crucial events upon which the whole growth or decline of a particular form of dance may have turned, and finding reasons why these things have happened, form the substance of dance history. Understanding of the dance is thereby illuminated. It is not confined to events long lost in the mists of antiquity but provides a context for the immediate dance situation, informs present knowledge and helps in the making of sound judgements of the nature, status and function of dance as well as its structure and performance.

Dance consists simply in the making of a form of structured movement which is given existence through performance and appraisal. The manipulation of movement in the making of a unique dance is perhaps *the* most crucial factor since without it there would be no 'dance', no choreography. Nonetheless written scores exist which, while they accurately represent the movements of the dance and demonstrate their relatedness, are not normally taken to be the dance. The dance is usually said to exist when it is *performed* by dancers, whether trained as such, or by ordinary people as in the case of social dances. The process of *appraisal* is continuous with both these acts of making the dance and of dancing, since without it they could not be brought to life. At its most basic it involves being critically aware, as a performer or choreographer, of the effect of each movement as it succeeds the previous one, and of the relation between movements in the progression to the completed whole.

Choreography

A historical examination of a specific dance might look at the *structural components* of the form, the movements, the sections of the dance, the accompanying elements of music, design, etc., and evaluate change through the time during which it was performed.

The different versions of a dance such as *Les Sylphides* would be a good example here since it has appeared in many guises.

Much of the evidence of actual dances of the past – the steps, the order of the movements, the amount of time they took, the spatial pattern they described, the accompaniment, and so on – is fragmentary and one is left with what might be called the 'dance residue'. This dance residue, together with other contemporary written and visual sources, is the basis for analysis, interpretation and, ultimately, the reconstruction of the dance.

A historical examination of the *choreographic process* might be concerned with how methods of working with movement in making dance have developed, as a matter of fact and as a matter of choreographers' reportage of psychological processes in creative work. A historical examination of individual *choreographers* might focus on them as people who are products of a specific artistic and social culture, or on the personal stamp they put on a repertoire of works to create a distinctive expressive style. In each case the focus of interest is different although the study is still of dances and those who make them. Similarly, the methods of procedure for undertaking a study of this kind would vary *in consequence of* the nature of the concern. To summarise, historical consideration of choreography might focus on an individual choreographer, on her/his repertoire, on the range of movements which characterise dances made by a number of choreographers in a certain historical period, on the use of properties, lighting and sound, in the types of structure used in giving form to a dance and on the theme and apparent meanings of dances.

Performance

In the area of *dance performance* two major strands of study emerge. One concerns the range and type of practical skills that are required in order that any one dance can actually be given existence. Clearly, those required for folk dance differ considerably from those of classical ballet. To be even more specific, they vary between one folk dance and another, between one classical ballet and another. The historical development of these technical skills in relation to changing choreographic demands would form a fascinating study.

The second major strand is the oft-neglected aspect of interpretation. A performance of a set (already choreographed) dance, whether in the theatre or in social life, offers by virtue of requiring

8

people to do it *an* interpretation of that dance. Other people might perform it differently. Lest confusion should arise here, there are several different senses in which the term 'interpretation' is used. The choreographic structure may be more or less specific, thus there may be little opportunity for the performer to introduce individual variation or there may be considerable freedom. The director of a performance deliberately selects a particular set of stylistic conventions in performance, as a conductor does in music, and an interpretation of the dance is given which may be clearly distinguishable from that of another director, producer or reconstructor.

Two caveats are necessary: firstly, that there is not an unlimited number of possible valid interpretations (see Best 1980) and, secondly, that an interpretation should not be confused with the idiosyncratic movement habits of performers. An interpretation is a considered portrayal of the dance based on extensive knowledge of the choreographer's repertoire and of the stylistic conventions of the period in which it was made.

In yet another sense, a spectator may also place a certain interpretation on what is seen and this involves the perception of events and of relationships between them within the whole pattern of the dance as it is given life through performance.

In all these examples there is scope for historical investigation which would considerably enrich understanding of dance in performance. Although there are difficulties in obtaining detailed descriptions and in reconstructing dances of the more distant past, studies are emerging which manage to do this (see Hilton 1981). To take a more recent example, the many different productions of Tudor's *Dark Elegies* would bear fruitful examination from its first performance in 1937 by the Ballet Rambert, to the 1980s performances by the Royal Ballet and Ballet Rambert.

Appreciation

The third area, *dance appreciation*, is concerned with making appraisals. The purpose of the process of appreciation is to examine the appropriateness of elements to the whole and to examine the value and significance of individual dances. The choreographer and the performer are both involved in this process in giving life to the dance while it is the particular concern of the professional critic whose writings are also of value as historical source material. The identification of salient features of the dance may itself have a historical variable in that its observable features may remain constant, but what is perceived to be *significant* about a dance may change through time. It may be hailed or damned for some innovatory, unconventional feature at its first performance and evaluated quite differently thirty or even three years later, should it survive. Commonalities of view might prove just as interesting as dissimilarities for the light they cast on the enduring value of particular dances.

In a wider sense appreciation covers more than the judgements made of individual dances and extends to choreographic styles, to genres and, ultimately, to an evaluation of any manifestation of dance within its own context. Dance traditions may be appraised for their efficacy in a social sense, as well as an artistic one, and this appraisal may itself change through the years.

1.4 *Genre, style and structure*

The precise nature of the *movement elements* which are present in a particular dance immediately locate it within a category of dances. A 'form' or 'genre' of dance, such as ballet or modern or jazz or folk, can be described as such because it is a composite of a large number of elements drawn together to make a distinctive dance form. Within these broad categories many sub-categories exist and boundaries will be blurred at many points. It is often only with hindsight, with the passage of time, that it becomes clear that a new genre has emerged. In the present time it may be problematic whether to label a dance as a 'modern ballet' or a 'contemporary dance' with precision. The desire to do this is not just for the sake of tying labels but because in order to understand dance it has to be placed within a relevant framework. At the greater extreme it becomes obvious that classical ballet, for example, is a clearly distinct genre from jazz dance. From this recognition a host of points follow. Questions about the historical and social origins of a form, of the reasons for its development, of the attitudes of those who dance and watch, can then be tackled.

Style and structure are two of the ideas which link across the three concepts of choreography, performance and appreciation and locate specific differences between dances. The *style* of a dance refers to the manner in which the subject matter of the dance is treated, in movement terms, and to the distinctive individual style of the person who made it, the choreographer. The ways in which dances are *structured*, how the phrases are put together in sections (if indeed they have sections) are further considerations which are central to the notion of choreography. Questions of genre, style and structure are relevant to all dances, and to focus on these aspects can draw attention either to the detail of the dance, or more widely, to its historical situation.

Each of the notions of choreography, performance and appreciation is a complex of interrelated strands. The further ideas, of genre, style and structure, relate across all three concepts and, in an important sense, help to focus attention on detailed aspects of the making of dance, the dancing and the appreciating in any specific instance.

1.5 *The place of the historical study of dance in education*

Although any individual may engage in dance history, it is studied in a more formal sense in educational institutions, although not to any great extent. One reason for the dearth of dance history courses is the prevailing emphasis on practical work which, until recent years, constituted the major part of dance courses both in schools and colleges. In some cases practical dance has been the *only* dance involvement offered to children. This is hardly surprising since teachers have had little background in dance history in their initial training whether this has been in the private or the state sectors of dance education.

The teaching of dance history has sometimes met with opposition and frequently with little enthusiasm because of a lack of awareness of the possibilities and excitement that exist. However, the introduction of C.S.E. (Certificate of Secondary Education) dance courses in 1966 and now of the new London University G.C.E. (General Certificate of Education) 'O' Level Dance syllabus, due to have its first examination in 1983, has brought with it greater appreciation of what might be taught. The A.E.B. (Associated Examining Board) G.C.E. 'O' Level Ballet syllabus, which has been taught mainly to pupils in privately financed schools since 1968, has had an extensive 'history of dance' section while the new G.C.E. Dance focuses on the period from 1870 to the present day.

In higher education institutions most courses in the history of dance have tended to be simple chronological accounts of dance from so-called 'primitive' man to the present day. The inadequacy of the typical twenty-hour history course which attempts to cover several centuries and a number of forms of dance has been demonstrated elsewhere (see Adshead 1981). There is little evidence of scholarly structure to support these courses. In colleges and polytechnics students may obtain degrees in which dance studies play a minor or a major part, and within these there is usually an area of study called the history of dance although the depth of such courses depends on a variety of factors. It may depend on the time available, the expertise of the teaching staff and the views held about dance and what is involved in its study.

Notwithstanding the fact that the study of dance history is already in existence (however minimally in many places), it is worth emphasising that the value of an understanding of the historical development of dance rests on the same grounds as that for any other area of human activity. Any activity has a history and the study of this history locates the activity within the wider framework of the society in which it originates.

There is a danger that learning how to do history, learning about historical events and broad cultural trends in various societies, may distort the study of dance by taking the focus away from the dance itself. In this case, history, rather than dance, becomes the major area of study. The problem is shared with many other subjects where disciplines such as history, anthropology and sociology may help to illuminate certain contextual matters. When the subject under study is as transient and ephemeral as dance, the difficulty is more pronounced. It is easy to be sidetracked into historical studies which look at social, political and artistic developments within the culture as a whole and which fail ever to look at the dance itself, its compositional structure and components, its performance requirements and how these have changed through time. A model for historical study which starts from dance is less likely to be at fault in this way. At higher levels of scholarship a dance historian will, of course, be almost as knowledgeable about history as about dance, but in school and college education in the early stages of studying dance history the purpose must be first and foremost to give students an appreciation of *dance, as historically situated.*

The view that one holds of the place and relevance of historical studies within dance education will depend, ultimately, upon the view one has of what education is about and what the study of dance is concerned with in that context. One might argue that practical participation is of greatest value. This itself can be further divided into dancing, making dances and appreciating them, OR one might consider that learning about dance is most informative, OR perhaps that some combination of the two is likely to lead to deeper understanding. It is consistent with the growth of dance in education during the twentieth century that the emphasis should have been predominantly upon participation since its adoption under the auspices of physical education depended upon justifications related to personal involvement, physical and emotional development, and social competence. The resultant orientation was towards dance as a physical activity, as relaxation from theoretical work, as a means of catharsis and of self-expression, rather than as a serious subject of study. In some senses this reflects the justifications operating in the world at large for the arts when they are seen primarily as entertainment. Going to the theatre is often seen to function in this way although serious artists and theatre-goers expect greater rewards in terms of the illumination of social problems or presentation of artistic statements of some significance.

In an education in dance, as in music and art, one would expect a depth of structural analysis and a notion of historical perspective as well as personal experience of the materials involved. In total, the purpose must be to deepen appreciation and understanding of dance in any style or form.

A development of these ideas about historical studies within the dance curriculum is given in Chapter 10. A specific example of a study unit of dance history is taken and the content and methods examined.

1.6 *Learning processes in the study of dance history*

It is useful in this context to distinguish between
1. learning *about dance* by studying texts, scores, etc.,
2. learning *to dance* and to *make dances,*
3. learning to appraise or *appreciate* dances according to suitable criteria in order to *make judgements.*

There are many accounts of the history of dance and an increasing number of notated scores, which are examples of the first kind of learning. It is possible to learn to perform some of the dances of different historical periods and to study interpretive requirements in this way as well as to create pieces 'in the style' of choreographers of the past. The third area, of making critical judgements of the dance and its literature, proceeds through the accepted academic methods of description, analysis, interpretation and evaluation. To look at reviews or accounts of dance within the prevailing notions of 'beauty' or 'line', etc., of the time is to appreciate the dance historically.

Expansion of the notion of the processes of learning and of methodologies which are appropriate for a particular study is found in Chapters 3, 10 and 11.

Summary

The type of historical dance study described in this chapter is a different enterprise from that of watching the latest dance craze on the television, or of going to the theatre to be entertained, or to see classical ballet or modern dance for artistic reasons. It is also different from training to be a dancer. It has its own standards and notions of excellence derived from scholarly historical dance study. It can be argued that the study of dance history is not a luxury to be indulged when time permits, nor is it a poor relation to the actual practice of making new dances and performing them. Dance history constitutes a valid study in its own right and an absolutely essential perspective in a dance education. Even the most avant-garde of the 'modern' dancers, by virtue of their titles and their dance concerns, acknowledge the past and place themselves, historically.

References

Adshead, J. 1981 *The study of dance*. London: Dance Books
Best, D. 1980 'The objectivity of artistic appreciation', *British Journal of Aesthetics*, vol. 20, no.2. (Spring 1980), pp. 115–27
Hilton, W. 1981 *Dance of court and theatre: The French noble style, 1690–1725*. London: Dance Books

CHAPTER 2

Methods in the historical study of dance

by June Layson

In this chapter the various ways of setting about the study of and, ultimately, research in dance history are discussed; the different processes that are used and the particular skills that have to be acquired are described. This is followed by a brief consideration of some of the outcomes of the study of dance history and a characterisation of what counts as good historical communication.

Dance historians, no less than other historians, need to develop particular working methods and procedures in their study if both the *process* – that is the doing, the finding out – and the *product* – which might be a folder, an essay or dance presentation – are to be profitable and worthwhile. Historians are like detectives in the sense that they deal with various *kinds of evidence or source material* in order to try to find out the truth, what really happened. It is only when the facts have been established and described that they can be analysed and interpreted.

2.1 *Primary and secondary source materials*

Firstly, it is important to distinguish between *primary* and *secondary source material* because this will determine the nature, the outcome and the value of the work. *Primary sources* are those that came into existence during the period being studied and thus they are first hand, contemporary and provide the raw material for dance study. Examples of primary source materials in dance would be a dance performance, a choreographer's working score or log with all its amendments and annotations, actual costumes worn by dancers for known performances of particular works and eye-witness accounts of certain dance events. *Secondary sources*, as the term suggests, are second hand, after the event accounts, often using hindsight to trace developments in the dance over a chosen span of time. All the standard dance histories, dance encyclopedias and dance reference books come into this category. Some of these texts are based on primary sources though the more 'popular' history paperbacks often use material previously published in other dance history books.

Some source material can be regarded as both primary and secondary according to the purposes for which it is being used. An example of this is the Kinney and Kinney (1914) dance history book which is a primary source of the immediate pre-1914 period; but during that time it functioned as a secondary source since the authors reviewed the development of dance from ancient Egypt up to the first decade or so of the twentieth century by reference to other published works.

The relative importance of primary and secondary sources usually depends upon the kind of work being done and the person undertaking it. The beginner, faced with too many primary sources at once, may be confused by apparently conflicting evidence, but to use only secondary sources could engender the attitude that all the interesting work has been done and dance history is fixed, undisputed and boring. The exclusive use of primary sources is the mark of the experienced dance researcher who refers to good secondary sources to provide background, points of entry for further study, bases of comparison, and so on. On the other hand, concentrating solely on secondary source material by reading many dance history books can be rewarding, interesting and informative, but as such this means reading about dance history, not getting involved in the methodologies of dance history nor actually contributing to it.

Generally then, a balance has to be maintained between the use of *primary* and *secondary* source materials that is appropriate to the kind of study being undertaken and this must be based on the recognition that the former are *of* a particular period and the latter are *about* a particular period, that the former were produced *during* the period and the latter *after* the period.

2.2 *The location of source materials*

Being able to differentiate between primary and secondary evidence is important in *locating source material*. Of course much source material has already been identified and collated and is readily available through the catalogues and collections of local and national libraries and museums. A recent example of this was the 1981 'Spotlight' exhibition mounted by the Theatre Museum at the Victoria and Albert Museum in London which showed a striking collection of dance costumes – all, in the dance history sense, primary source material. Nevertheless, the evidence being sought is often missing and has to be searched for, and this may entail fieldwork. One of the early skills that has to be acquired is that of knowing the most likely and profitable places where a particular piece of evidence might be located. In studying dance history this could involve visiting a nearby library to read through back copies of local newspapers in order to find out whether a certain dance event, such as a celebratory social ball, is described; or it might entail sifting through a collection of photographs of a specific dance production in order to gain information on costume details. Locating historical evidence about dance needs patience and ingenuity. The chance sighting in a back copy of an early twentieth century magazine of an advertisement placed by a dancing master may be the first clue in a quest to find the answers to such questions as, What kind of dance did he teach? Whom did he teach? Where? It may be necessary to make visits to nearby Assembly Rooms or country mansions to find out how certain physical situations such as the size of the room, the type of floor, the area set aside for musicians may have affected the dances that from written sources are known to have taken place there. Similarly, talking and, more importantly, listening to elderly people who can remember past local dance festivals or the dance-crazes of their youth can be another fascinating way of gathering evidence and gaining access to dance history.

Being able to locate source materials is therefore crucial for the dance historian and this involves not only using libraries and museums but also identifying other, usually more local, sources that might be profitable.

2.3 *Categories of source materials*

Once found, the evidence or source material may be incomplete, puzzling or even contradictory. Indeed each piece of evidence needs to be cross-checked against other evidence and at this point it is essential to be able to sort the material, be it primary or secondary, into different *categories*.

Dance material can be placed in various categories such as written (theatre programmes) and non-written (photographs); public (newspaper review articles) and private (dancers' diaries and letters), and so on. The point is that whatever category is adopted it should help the dance historian's study by enabling like material to be grouped together and also by acting as a checklist which might indicate further areas to be investigated.

The categories proposed here are broad and would need to be subdivided according to the particular focus of the study being undertaken but they provide a preliminary basis and reflect the format used in many dance archives and collections. Note that individual sources are listed alphabetically rather than in order of importance, the latter being determined by the focus of any particular study. The items listed are not mutually exclusive, an overlap being inevitable in some cases.

1. Written sources – advertisements, autobiographies, bills, cast lists, choreographers' log books, critics' reviews, dance notations, diaries, edicts, journals, letters, literature, magazines, music notations, newspapers, parish records, posters, school records, theatre programmes, receipts, tracts, etc.
2. Visual sources – primarily the dance itself, also architecture, costumes, designs for sets, films, musical instruments, paintings, photographs, prints, properties, sculpture, videotapes, etc.
3. Aural sources – music, live and recorded, taped interviews and reminiscences, etc.

The above lists are by no means exhaustive, indeed it is unlikely that definitive lists could be drawn up since different kinds of materials may be of value to the dance historian in different circumstances. The predominance of *written sources* reflect their vital role in all historical study but in dance history it is necessary to use these in conjunction with *visual and aural sources* if a comprehensive view of the dance of a period is to be gained. This is certainly the case in working with early dance notation scores. An attempt to reconstruct from the Feuillet notation a particular gavotte performed at the beginning of the eighteenth century would of necessity involve reference to other contemporary written, visual and aural sources in order to achieve some degree of accuracy in steps, style, manner and quality.

The dance as a *visual source* in its own right is often taken for granted yet certain dances, even in the here and now of performance, are 'living history'. It was the recognition of this fact that prompted Cecil Sharp at the beginning of this century to start collecting the traditional dances of Great Britain and then to pursue this work in the U.S.A. where he and his assistants found that many of the seventeenth century Playford dances were still being performed by descendants of the early British settlers. Similarly, a current performance of one of the classical ballets such as *Swan Lake* is but the latest presentation of a work that originated in 1877 and, even though the choreography has changed perhaps almost totally, its survival today is a modern manifestation of a dance form of considerable historical significance. Thus a dance performance may itself contain the historical threads which can be traced back from the present through time to its inception or earliest records.

2.4 *Problematic source materials*

Although most of the items in the three categories could readily be labelled as primary source material, some present problems in determining their primary or secondary status. Descriptions of village dance festivals and society balls often occur in historical novels and appear to be authentic. Nevertheless, such literature needs to be treated with caution since it is primary source material only for the period *in* which it was written and it cannot be regarded as evidence for the period *about* which it was written. There are, for example, several references to dance in Hardy's *Under the Greenwood Tree* (1872) which prompted the then English Folk Dance Society to write to Hardy in 1926 and enquire about the accuracy of his dance descriptions. Hardy replied that in this novel he was describing a 'six-hands round country dance' that he had 'last danced sixty years ago'. In this particular instance, therefore Hardy was placing a remembered personal experience (primary source) in a novel set in the early nineteenth century (fictional context).

Another problem that occurs with written material is in the use of translations. Historical studies of dance forms that cross language boundaries necessitate using translations if the texts cannot be read in their original form. Often translations are made by non-dancers and then the dance essence of the work may be in jeopardy but even when bilingual dance experts such as Horst Koegler and Walter Sorell undertake a translation it must be remembered that some dance terms and nuances are not readily translatable.

Drawings, paintings, prints, sculptures and sketches of dancers by contemporary artists may at first sight be considered good primary source material; however, this is to ignore prevailing artistic conventions and style. In her book *The dance in Ancient Greece*, Lawler (1964) points to the consequence of not recognising such conventions in art.

> The Greek vase painter often draws figures without a 'floor line' – a convention which has led some modern interpreters to insert an imaginary 'floor line' of their own in a given scene, and then to deduce from its position all sorts of untenable conclusions, e.g. that the ancient Greeks engaged in something like ballet and even toe-dancing.
>
> (p.21)

Lawler gives several further examples which show how necessary it is to treat such material with caution and more especially the dangers of using it as an exact record upon which to base a dance reconstruction. Even when it is known that a dancer cooperated with or posed for an artist, as in Isadora Duncan's case, it is necessary to realise that what is presented is seen through the artists' eyes. Sketches by Rodin and Bourdelle of Duncan dancing are so different in the impression they give of the dynamism of Duncan's movement – the former being more static and robust, the latter being more fluid and delicate – that in this sense they are akin to secondary source material.

In the light of the difficulties that may arise in the use of visual works of art it might be assumed that photographs and films of dancers would be accurate and, consequently, impeccable source material. However, this would not allow for the fact that many of the technical problems encountered in the early days of photography and film, such as exposure time and capturing movement accurately, were not solved until well into the twentieth century. Thus photographs of Fanny Cerrito (c. 1855) were of necessity posed, as are most of those of Denishawn dancers taken between 1915 and 1931. Therefore, in using photographs as historical evidence it is important to distinguish between posed and action photographs, and to establish location. Posed portraits are usually taken in the photographer's studio, although occasionally outdoor and theatre locations are used, and the pose may or may not be from an actual dance. Action photographs, a comparatively recent development, may evoke a performance mood and quality, but even when captioned with the title of a dance it does not necessarily follow that such photographs were taken during an actual performance.

Similar problems emerge when audio-tapes of conversations are used for dance study. A recorded interview with a choreographer about a new work would be categorised as a primary aural source, but a 1983 recording of a former dancer reminiscing about Diaghilev would best be regarded as a primary aural source to be used with great care and caution since memory is not infallible and in retrospect events can be re-organised, rationalised and re-interpreted. Such recalled evidence needs to be cross-checked with reliable contemporary accounts.

2.5 *Evaluation of source materials*

Having located, assembled and categorised the various dance sources, the next stage is to evaluate them by differentiating between '*witting*' and '*unwitting*' *testimony* (see Marwick 1970) and by applying tests of *authenticity, reliability* and *value*.

The term '*witting*' *testimony* is used to describe those primary sources in which the originator of the source set out intentionally to convey the information that the source contains. Examples of witting testimony abound in dance history. Macdonald (1975), in her study of Diaghilev, focuses her entire text on the writings of dance critics, an instance where witting testimony is used with considerable effect. In contrast, Sachs (1933, trans. 1937) bases his classification of dance themes and types on the reports of European travellers who, from the seventeenth century onwards, saw various kinds of tribal dancing in the then remote areas of Africa, Asia and other parts of the world. However, sometimes these eye-witnesses to the event give information over and above what they intended and this is then termed '*unwitting*' *testimony*. In some of the accounts included by Sachs the use of words such as 'obscene' and 'hideous' conveys more about the attitudes of the European onlookers than the quality of the dance being described. Indeed, it is often this very failure to realise the culture-bound stance of observers and to ignore the unwitting nature of their testimony that makes the early dance history texts both suspect and difficult to use. An example of an author who uses statements about dance for both their witting and unwitting testimony is Rust (1969), much of whose work is derived from teenagers' views on types of social dance current in the 1960s.

Although eye-witness and participant accounts readily provide examples of both witting and unwitting testimony other kinds of primary source material can be regarded as testimony of some sort. Thus the publications of the Board of Education (1909) and the Gulbenkian Foundation (1980) both make witting statements about the dance of their time. In contrast many of the photographs of women dancers taken during the first quarter of this century provide unwitting evidence which the dance historian can use to gain insight into the then prevailing attitudes to the body and to women. Most of the dancers are plump, even fat by today's standards, and many of their poses appear coy, arch or 'pretty'.

Problems of *authenticity* are occasionally encountered by a dance historian. Modern examples of this are Nijinsky's (1937) diaries and Duncan's (1927) autobiography, since both publications have been questioned on the grounds of authenticity. It has been suggested that the original writings of these dancers have been amended and altered and in some instances passages written by others inserted. However, unless the historical study is based on only one source, and this would be rare, questions of authenticity can usually be resolved or at least allowed for by reference to other similar primary sources.

The *reliability* or the degree to which a particular source can be trusted is an important factor in studying the history of dance. A dance theatre programme listing choreographers and giving credits for the design of sets and costumes, sound accompaniment and lighting can normally be relied upon as giving accurate information. Nevertheless, when dancers are injured, last minute alterations in casting and even in the dances presented may have to be made and therefore what is printed regarding certain dances and performers in a theatre programme may not always be accurate. This point is recognised by Bland (1981) in the notes to the 'Statistics' section of his book on the Royal Ballet where he writes:

sources for castings are the nightly programmes corrected, as far as possible, from Stage Management records or eye-witness accounts.

(p.264)

The *value* of a single item of source material and the comparative value of several source materials may depend upon the nature and scope of the historical study being undertaken. Shawn's (1910) book on Delsarte, the movement theorist, is itself a secondary source but since Delsarte did not publish his own work and the publications of his various pupils are not all readily available in this country, Shawn's text is often used in the study of Delsarte's theories. It is important therefore to establish the value of Shawn's book as a means of gaining access to Delsarte's work. In this case, as in many others, the matter may be resolved to a large extent by examining the bibliography and the references cited. Mere length in either case does not guarantee worth, but in Shawn's thirty-six page bibliography the Delsarte literature itemised consists almost entirely of primary sources and the annotations are particularly detailed. This is an indication of the book's value as good secondary source material to the dance historian studying Delsarte.

With some written material the value of the evidence it contains can be determined by relevant knowledge of the author and this is particularly so in using the work of the dance critics. Dance criticism at its best is objective and informative, with the judgements made being supported explicitly by reasons and by reference to the choreography, the performance, and so on. However, this is not always the case as when, for example, Arnold Haskell's enthusiasm for certain dancers bursts through his writing. Although dance critics may well enthuse and inspire, it is important in the study of dance history to be able to recognise the difference between matters of fact and matters of personal opinion in their writings. On the other hand Cyril Beaumont's (1970) perplexed remark to Roose-Evans on first seeing Martha Graham dance in *Appalachian Spring* in 1954: 'but why does she roll about on the floor . . .? It breaks the line' (p. 110) is only understandable in the light of the knowledge that Beaumont was an expert on ballet rather than modern dance. His remark as such is of little value to the dance historian trying to analyse Graham's choreography but it could be of considerable value to a dance historian interested in, for example, the development of different modes of dance criticism.

2.6 *Use of source materials*

Whatever the reason for historical study, be it to reconstruct a dance, to provide background information for a production, to write a dissertation or solely to gain knowledge and understanding, a point is reached when the assembled and categorised source materials have to be used. This is the stage of *making sense of the materials*, of pooling the evidence to see the overall picture and of discerning emerging patterns and trends.

If the source materials are to be the basis for dance reconstruction or used in some form of production or performance, then the work will inevitably become more and more practical as the various pieces of evidence are put together, acted upon and tried out. The length of this process depends upon the degree of accuracy required, but it is inevitable that the source material will be referred to frequently with much checking and cross-checking. Often the working out process itself reveals further information in the source material that was not immediately recognised as such in the initial study. Sometimes it indicates gaps in the evidence which might be filled by locating more specific sources or have to be bridged by using what is available in an imaginative way, though such conjecture would need to be undertaken with care. The practical outcomes of historical study may be varied but the derivation from source material, while not necessarily being obvious, gives the work its historical worth and merit.

If the source materials are to be used as the basis for some form of written historical work* then the 'making sense of' process usually proceeds along well defined lines. It may be appropriate to describe all the source materials collected, although a chronicle of dance events or a catalogue of facts about dance would not normally constitute historical study. Nevertheless, the first listing of all a choreographer's works in the form of a choreochronicle derived from primary source materials would be regarded as a significant piece of historical work.

Usually, however, the source material is taken as a whole and is presented in the form of an overview with the main features of the area described and reference made to individual sources where

*The planning and writing of historical studies is discussed in detail in Chapter 11.

relevant. After a descriptive section most written historical studies embark upon a process of analysis in which the material is interpreted and explained. The intention is to present a balanced and reasoned argument which gives as complete a picture as possible of the dance within the selected historical context.

2.7 *Characteristics of good historical communication*

The form in which the results of a historical study of dance are presented may vary from a performance to a dissertation but the characteristics of such communication are very similar. Good historical communication is based on the careful use of primary and esteemed secondary sources which are acknowledged in the final work whether it be in the performance of a reconstructed dance or as in-text references in a written study. It is these source materials that are related, analysed and then used to produce worthwhile statements about and insights into the dance of the past.

The reason for undertaking study in the history of dance and then communicating the results is to attempt to answer, at least in part, the crucial questions: Who danced? What did they dance? How? Where? Why? Having proposed answers to such questions, the dance historian is then in a position to indicate changes in dance through time, to highlight important features and to explain the factors underlying certain events.

The degree to which any historical study of dance contributes to the sum total of knowledge about dance depends almost entirely upon *what* sources are used and the *methods* employed in working with them.

In Chapter 3 various dance history books are described and evaluated in terms of the types of source material selected and the working methods used.

References

Bland, A. 1981 *The Royal Ballet – the first fifty years.* London: Threshold
Board of Education 1909 *The syllabus of physical exercise for schools 1909.* London: H.M.S.O.
Duncan, I. 1927 *My life.* New York: Boni and Liveright
Gulbenkian Foundation 1980 *Dance education and training in Britain*
Hardy, T. 1872, 1974 *Under the Greenwood Tree.* London: Macmillan

Kinney, T. & Kinney, M. W. 1914, 1936 *The dance: Its place in art and life.* New York: Tudor

Lawler, L. 1964 *The dance in Ancient Greece.* London: A. & C. Black

Macdonald, N. 1975 *Diaghilev observed by critics in England and the United States, 1911–1929.* London: Dance Books

Marwick, A. 1970 *The nature of history.* London: Macmillan

Nijinsky, V. (ed.) 1937 Romola Nijinsky, *The diary of Valsav Nijinsky.* London: Gollancz

Roose-Evans, J. 1970 *Experimental theatre.* London: Studio Vista

Rust, F. 1969 *Dance in society.* London: Routledge & Kegan Paul

Sachs, C. 1933, trans. 1937 *World history of the dance.* New York: Norton

Shawn, T. 1910, 1963 *Every little movement.* New York: Dance Horizons

CHAPTER 3

Studies in dance history

by Janet Adshead

3.1 Dance
- 3.1.1 General histories of dance spread widely over time and place
- 3.1.2 General histories of an era and/or type of dance
- 3.1.3 Specific studies of a type of dance within a short period of time
- 3.1.4 Historical accounts of the emergence of new forms of dance

3.2 People
- 3.2.1 Accounts of the life and work of notable figures in dance history
- 3.2.2 Collected writings of choreographers, performers and theorists
- 3.2.3 Collected writings of dance critics

3.3 Companies
- 3.3.1 Histories of dance companies
- 3.3.2 Guides to the current repertoire, works placed in historical context

3.4 Contemporary literature
- 3.4.1 Historical accounts of the dance in the literature of a period

The materials of dance history – that is, the sources of evidence of the existence of dance through time – can be categorised and used in many different ways. In Chapter 2 a full account is given of the range of source materials available and of the potential values and problems of using them to acquire understanding of the dance of the past. In later chapters specific types of sources are taken as the starting point for work in dance history (see Chapters 4, 5 and 6 which refer to the use of journals, company archives and regional documents). In the present chapter some dance history books are described both as *examples of specific types of historical study*, in relation to the framework outlined in Chapter 1. and as *examples of the use of the particular kinds of source materials* described in Chapter 2. These texts are also valuable resources for introducing students to dance history.

To attempt comprehensive coverage of all the available dance history texts would be an enormous undertaking and would be unrealistic in this context. The selection of a limited number of books is, therefore, necessary if somewhat difficult. The reasons for the selection made here are several.

Firstly, these texts are good examples of *types* of dance history study in which one can see the approaches outlined earlier particularly well-defined. Thus the procedures and materials required for the various kinds of study proposed in the previous chapter can be seen in practical use. Different lines of investigation become clear in relation to the nature of the topic being pursued. Certain limitations are also consequent upon the choice of topic and the manner of dealing with it and these, too, become obvious.

Secondly, some categories of historical writing are virtually omitted, e.g. straightforward biographies and autobiographies, although these sources exist and are of value. Anyone embarking on a detailed study of a particular individual would, of course, read their autobiography and/or biography and those of contemporary artists. The biographies included here are ones which place emphasis on the work of the person rather than on their private lives.

Additionally, the writings of important individuals in the history of dance are available in a different form, drawn together in collections, e.g. by Brown (1980) and Cohen (1974), and these texts provide primary sources of reference across a long time span. As a starting point in the study of dance history these texts are perhaps of greater importance than the biography or autobiography of a single individual.

Thirdly, a further type of dance history is not represented at all. This is the dance history of cultures other than those of Europe and the U.S.A. There are two main reasons for this: the small amount of historical dance scholarship of this kind that is neither superficial nor patronising;* the predominant emphasis within the study of dance history at the present time on dance as a theatrical form and, to a lesser extent, as a social activity. The selection of texts reflects the current state of affairs while not condoning it. Any aspect of dance has its history, an appropriate methodology for studying it and a value of its own.

Fourthly, the books surveyed here are standard works which are generally available. All the texts are accessible to the public through bookshops and libraries. A specialist dance bookshop (such as Dance Books, London) would obtain any published text on dance. Further list of books, journals, bibliographic sources, dictionaries, encyclopedias, etc., can be found in Appendix A.

The texts presented here are divided into a number of categories and the orientation and main concerns of each given in columns on the following pages with a brief summary and discussion. In the first column the full title and publication details can be found. In the second and third columns the time span and geographical range is noted so that the extent of the work in time and place is clear. In the fourth column the overall scope of the work and its major aims, purposes and concerns are identified. A statement of the parameters of the enquiry and area of investigation is helpful in assessing the value of the book since it has to be judged in terms of what it sets out to do. The sources on which it is based are characterised in column five and its structure and content in column six. The structure of the book might be seen to be chronological or thematic, to take an extended period of time or to concentrate on a short period. The contents of the text are briefly outlined. The seventh column contains an evaluation of the book and suggests its possible uses in the study of the history of dance.

3.1 *Dance*

3.1.1 *General histories of dance spread widely over time and place*
The main feature of a general history of dance is its long time span. It is also likely to range widely through geographical space, although study of the more recent centuries tends to receive detailed attention,

---

*There are a few notable exceptions to the first point, and one of these is Ranger's text (1975) on the Beni dance of East Africa, set within a sociohistorical perspective.

3.1.1. General histories of dance spread widely over time and place

Title	Time span	Geographical range	Scope and major concerns	Sources used
Sachs, C. *World history of the dance* N.Y.: Norton 1933, trans. 1937	Antiquity–present	Worldwide	History of the dance worldwide, illustrating themes common to the dance and its movement characteristics	Standard C19th anthropological theories, travellers' tales, mainly primary sources
Sorell, W. *Dance in its time* N.Y.: Doubleday 1981	C12th–1960s	Europe and USA	Sociohistorical view of theatre dance, accounts for the development of dance in terms of the artistic, social and political climate	Standard histories e.g. Sachs, mainly secondary sources, but covering the context as well as the dance
Kraus, R. *History of the dance in art and education* N.J.: Prentice-Hall 1969	'Primitive' times to 1960s	Europe and USA	History of the cultural roles of dance, illustrates the emergence of contemporary theatre dance and dance in education	Secondary, derived from standard accounts, e.g. Sachs, Lawler, Backman, appropriately acknowledged. Primary sources on education in the USA
Quirey, B. *May I have the pleasure?* London: BBC 1976	Prehistory to 1976 mainly C17th–C20th	Western Europe, narrows to England	History of popular dancing written to accompany TV programmes, describes the dances and the style of performance with some sociohistorical background	Original writings of dancing masters, pictorial, verbal, musical and dance notation sources, as well as general histories
Backman, E.L. *Religious dances in the Christian Church and in popular medicine* Conn.: Greenwood 1952, 1972	Antiquity–C19th	Asia/Europe narrows to W. Europe including Scandinavia	History of religious and therapeutic uses of dance; traces outbreaks of dancing and relates them to theological dogma and medical practice	Original European and Scandinavian sources; theological, literary, legal and musical
Kirstein, L. *A short history of classical theatrical dancing* N.Y.: Dance Horizons 1935, 1942, 1969	Prehistory–1942	Western world narrows to USA	History of theatrical dancing, traces growth of dance in this context	Secondary sources in three languages used to illustrate detailed points Primary, first-hand account of the early part of the C20th

Structure and content	Evaluation
1. Common characteristics of dance, by types and themes 2. Chronological account of dances from the Stone Age to the C20th	*The* standard dance history. Its generality gives rise to misconceptions because of its unsubstantiated theoretical basis A broad picture of the multiplicity of dance forms emerges clearly
Chronological but under thematic headings e.g. C12th–C14th dance, 'The long awakening','Balletomania', 'Dance criticism and the era of Gautier'	A useful example of a sociohistorical account with little emphasis on the structure of the dance. General themes, parallels across forms emerge within a total picture of the dance A good introductory text
1. Chronological account from 'primitive' times, covering a wide variety of dance styles and relating dance to other arts 2. Two major sections on contemporary dance in the theatre in America and on dance education, a review of its aims, current practice and problems	A readable history, well illustrated which provides a good overview of the history of dance and of standard sources of information One of the few accounts of dance in education in C20th America and very useful from this point of view A good introductory text
1. The validity of evidence used in reconstructing dances of the past 2. General historical overview 3. C17th–C20th dances in detail, with descriptions of the steps and style of performance 4. Brief chronology of events; occupants of the thrones of England and France	A short book which provides a useful starting point, particularly for courses in dance history which have a practical element Reconstruction and interpretation are emphasised as is the consideration of the evidence upon which this is done
Chronological account but thematic within the broad structure e.g. The prohibition of religious dances The dance and the dead Choreomania and heresy	Detailed but readable account of the religious and therapeutic role of dance. Uncovers many strands of this complex area of study, demonstrates interwoven threads of myth, medical and religious dogma An original, well researched, definitive source
Chronological account emphasising the theatrical context of dance through myth and ritual of Rome and Egypt, the Middle Ages, the Court ballet, to C20th classical dance	A valuable source for adult/student beginners in dance history, using authentic evidence to good effect The broad sweep leads to generalisation and a certain bias towards the classical ballet means comments on modern dance should be treated with caution

and to focus on Western Europe. Problems concerning the lack of available evidence for dance in eras long gone perhaps leads writers to generalise across the few facts that are known in response to the question 'where did it all begin?'. A limitation in scope to one century or to a particular kind or function of dance, e.g. social dance, allows concentration on either a shorter period or on the form in greater depth. It also may produce a more detailed account of the function of dance in that period, while still retaining the width of a general historical account.

3.1.2. *General histories of an era and/or type of dance*

In these four texts the width of the area of study is limited in different ways. In the book by Rust the focus is on those forms of dance which predominantly have had a social function and which existed within one country. The particular analysis that she used was the basis of an investigation of current dance practice and thus provides an example of a historically situated sociological analysis of dances performed in society at large. It is the social context of the dances that is important. Richardson limits his time span to *one century*, his dancers to those from the *upper strata of society*, and remains within a *single country*. He can then afford to describe the dances in greater detail and discuss the manner of performance – that is, to focus on who danced, what they danced and how, stylistically. He also relates these factors to the physical performance space.

Although the Stearns take a long time span they limit the study to a *continent* and to a *genre*, that of dancing to jazz in a vernacular style. Major historical developments within that style can then be pinpointed. Emery's account of black dance limits the enquiry by *race* and *continent* while taking note of origins in other areas of the world where this is of crucial importance.

In some senses Rust and Richardson stand in a similar relationship to each other as do the Stearns and Emery texts.

3.1.3 *Specific studies of a type of dance within a short period of time*

These studies of a specific type of dance within a clearly defined era in dance history are usually located in smaller geographical areas also. The time span is determined by significant events, although it may be obvious only with hindsight that a trend was changing or dramatically new forms emerging. Lawler's period is determined by the existence of a certain culture and she considers all the types of dance that existed during that era while Hilton's approach is to examine a distinctive style of dance and the techniques required for its performance. Her time and geographical span are determined by the period during which that style existed. Guest and Gautier both document the establishment of a new style of ballet, the Romantic Ballet. Guest does it as a historian and Gautier as a critic of the period. The two taken together provide first-hand accounts placed fully in historical perspective.

3.1.4 *Historical accounts of the emergence of new forms of dance*

These three texts have in common the beginnings of a culturally specific form of dance, the American modern dance of the twentieth century. In total they cover the time span from the middle of the eighteenth century, in searching for its roots, to the establishment of modern dance in the 1940s. All are concerned to pinpoint crucial reasons for the development of modern dance and to describe its major innovators and the works they produced. The time span is fairly short, the focus is on one emerging form of dance. In the main these authors are as much concerned with the people who choreographed and danced as with the works they produced.

3.2 *People*

3.2.1 *Accounts of the life and work of notable figures in dance history*

Many history of dance texts focus around the life of an important individual whose contribution to the evolution of dance is described. The person may be primarily a choreographer or a dancer, a critic or a theorist. The approach to this task may vary from a personal life history to a critical analysis of the work of that person through the eyes of the critics of that and subsequent periods.

Lynham and Shelton, writing on Noverre and St Denis respectively, present life stories in a chronological manner combin-

3.1.2. General histories of an era and/or a type of dance

Title	Time span	Geographical range	Scope and major concerns	Sources used
Rust, F. *Dance in society* London: R.K.P. 1969	Brief early history, C13th–1969	England	History of social dance and society, analyses changes in the dance in relation to class; sex differences; economic change	Standard sources in dance history, some primary material reproduced at length Original sociological analysis based on questionnaires
Richardson, P. *The social dances of the C19th in England* London: Jenkins 1960	C19th	England	Sociohistorical account of social dances, describes origins and traces change correlated to the social life of the time. Focus on who danced and what they danced	General sources from the period, technical descriptions from primary sources and dancing manuals of the time
Stearns, M. & J. *Jazz dance. The story of American vernacular dance* London: Macmillan 1964	Prehistory –1960s	USA	A history of dancing to jazz from its origins in Africa to present American forms, focus on genre and style from an analysis of steps	General histories, original material based on interviews with over 200 individuals Discusses problems of interpreting evidence and its validity Gives detailed notes
Emery, L. *Black dance in the U.S. from 1619–1970* Cal.: National 1972	C15th–1970	USA (Caribbean)	Sociohistorical account of black dance forms used by people of African origin	Detailed reference to previously unpublished primary material Extensive quotations

Structure and content	Evaluation
1. Overview of historical function of dance from an anthropological point of view	Structural/functionalist analysis of dance within a historical framework Dance presented as an integral part of culture, giving an indication of the many complex factors as they influence the dance
2. Functional analysis of different eras from C13th through Tudor and Elizabethan times to the C20th	A useful text for studying dance that has primarily a social function and for those contemplating any practical social study of dance forms
3. Discussion based on sociological hypothesis	
4. Report of original research study of attitudes to dance in contemporary society	
1. Description of the Assembly rooms as special places for dance in the late C18th and early C19th	Presents the general proposition that change in dance is brought about by changes in social life and that new dances start with the ordinary people and rise through the social scale
2. The dances performed in them with particular emphasis on the period to 1865	Detailed descriptions are combined with interesting anecdotes Some background knowledge probably required to make full use of this text
3. American influences of the later C19th	It offers discussion about reconstruction and possibilities for further studies of a similar kind
4. Characterisation of steps and dance programmes	
The whole is within the context of C18th influences, relating change in social life to general issues	
Chronological tracing of major developments in style through minstrel, carnival, circus, roadshow, tin pan alley, Broadway, tap, acrobatics, etc.	Substantial original study of a specific style of dance, well documented and entertainingly written Suitable as an example of a study of any kind of dance and particularly required for jazz and vernacular USA studies
Basic movements given in notation	
Chapters range from the early Slave Trade through Caribbean dance 1518–1900, Juba; minstrelsy; dance hall; to concert dance of the 1930–70 period	The social meanings of many forms of black dance are illuminated in their rightful context, i.e. the societies in which they occurred A very useful and well researched study, invaluable as a guide to any serious investigation of black dance
Uses meticulously referenced sources from contemporary accounts within the context of modern social and cultural theory	Exposes the bias of many accounts of slave owners and wealthy travellers

3.1.3. Specific studies of a type of dance within a short period of time

Title	Time span	Geographical range	Scope and major concerns	Sources used
Lawler, L. *The dance in Ancient Greece* Conn.: Wesleyan U.P. 1964	3,000 BC –527 AD	Ancient Greece	History of all types of dance occuring during this period; examines characteristics and functions	Original Greek sources listed and use discussed whether archeological, literary, etc. Discusses problems of interpretation
Hilton, W. *Dance of court and theatre. The French Noble style 1690–1725* London: Dance Books 1981	1690– 1725	France	History of a particular style of dancing, the French Noble style; analyses style, technique, and notation	Original sources from Louis XIV's dancing masters Discusses problems of reconstruction from the various kinds of evidence available, i.e. verbal, pictorial notation
Guest, I. *The Romantic Ballet in Paris* London: Pitman 1966	1820–47	Paris	History of a distinctive style within the genre of ballet, documents the emergence of ballet as a major theatre art in the Romantic Age	Based on the archives of the Paris Opera and on contemporary written sources in a number of languages Extensive notes; Appendix lists principal dancers 1820–47 and dances performed
Gautier, T. *The Romantic Ballet*, as seen by Theophile Gautier trans. from French by C. W. Beaumont London: Beaumont 1932	1837–48	Paris	Collected reviews over eleven years of the major dance critic of the period	Original views and reviews of performances of new works and revivals

Structure and content	Evaluation
Chronological: prehistoric; Mycenean; pre-classical; transition to Middle Ages	Excellent standard reference text for the period
Then by types of dances; animal dances; dances at shrines; mystery dances; dance and drama; dance and the people	Research results presented in a highly readable manner Illustrates the problems of pursuing studies of this kind where the dance itself no longer exists.
Discusses types of dance and their function for that society	
1. General background of court and theatre, place and type of dance, dancing masters and their publications	An example of the depth of study that is possible both in the area of perform-ance skills and interpretation of steps and in the problems of imagining/ reconstructing a dance style of the past
2. Analysis of the noble style and its notation	May be used as a manual of instruction for dances of the early C18th and as a theoretical analysis
3. Appendices of Labanotation for the steps, exercises for performance style, chronology of political events	A crucially important, highly detailed study of a very short period in dance history
4. Bibliography categorised into periods, countries; French, Italian, German and English sources both original and modern writings	
A chronological account of the emergence of the Romantic Style, from its origins in Noverre's work and taking account of the influence of notable artists in bringing about a more lyrical style	A valuable account of the sociohistorical context of the arts and of the distinctive heritage of the classical ballet Detailed research source book for the period but also a highly readable text which gives the lives of important individuals and stories of events
Discusses the dances, technique, scenic design and music	The short time span allows detail to be presented
Gives a detailed assessment of indi-viduals, e.g. Taglioni, Elssler	
1. Account of Gautier's life from 1811 to 1872 by Beaumont, as poet, journa-list, art and drama critic, writer of scenarios	A valuable original account of dance performed during this period, from the critic's point of view He places strong emphasis on the dancer rather than the structure of the dance but reveals the aesthetic prevailing at the time
2. Principal notices of performances given in Paris between 1837–48 with detailed descriptions of staging, cost-umes and dancers' physical attributes	
3. Gives both story lines and qualitative assessment of performance	

3.1.4. Historical accounts of the emergence of new forms of dance

Title	Time span	Geographical range	Scope and major concerns	Sources used
Ruyter, N.L. *Reformers and Visionaries: The Americanisation of the art of dance* N.Y.: Dance Horizons 1979	late C18th –mid C20th	USA	A history of the emergence of a distinctively American form of dance in the theatre and in education	Major collection of primary Delsarte material in English published between 1882–1913 Historical summaries based on primary sources
Kendall, E. *Where she danced* N.Y.: Knopf 1979	1845– 1930	USA	A history of two major figures in modern dance, Ruth St Denis and Martha Graham, and through them the growth of a new dance form	Sources not directly attributed in the text, but the whole based on scholarly work Reference to late C19th sources valuable
Magriel, P. (Ed.) *Chronicles of American Dance From the Shakers to Martha Graham* N.Y.: Da Capo 1948, 1978	mid C19th –1940s	USA	A history of dance from religious to theatrical forms in a specifically American style	Primary sources, newspaper criticisms, and reviews, e.g. of *The Black Crook* 1866–68

ing theories of the dance with choreographic and performance details in the context of the individuals evolving personal and social life. Buckle, on Diaghilev, is perhaps the most detailed account of this type providing an almost daily record.

Macdonald and Vaughan, on Diaghilev and Ashton respectively, detach themselves from the intimate life of the person and discuss their works through critical reviews. Vaughan's text is a much more elaborated account which uses quotations selectively while Macdonald produces verbatim the records of the time. Both are

Structure and content	Evaluation
1. General historical account of early theatre dance in the American social scene of the C18th and C19th. Detailed accounts of ballet; Delsarte; and early modern dancers such as Isadora Duncan and Ruth St Denis	An interesting account of the entry of dance into the mainstream of respectable life in education and the theatre and its acquisition of status in middle class culture
	The dance emerges through a study of personalities in two distinct manifestations, as art and as art in education
2. General historical account of educational theory in the C18th and C19th. Detailed account of dance education and its early development through the work of e.g. Colby, H'Doubler	A thematic study which would be best used after some background knowledge has been acquired
3. Valuable bibliography	

1. Ruth St Denis and her influence on health and beauty, the theatre, European art and Isadora Duncan	A highly readable account of dance as popular entertainment, as spectacular extravaganza in balletic style and as a serious art form
2. Developments in dance on the West Coast from Salome to Denishawn and Hollywood	The very early period is particularly of value
	Useful in attempting to answer the question of what gave the protagonists of modern dance the courage to insist that they had found a new art form
3. Martha Graham's emergence as a major artist	
4. Valuable bibliography	

Points to different precursors of the modern dance in religious forms (Shakers); show dance; minstrels; tap; theatrical spectacles; social dance academies; early ballet in the classic mode	Through a collection of readings and research articles by different authors Magriel draws together a history from religious and puritan origins through tap and minstrel forms as a context for the emergence of major personalities in modern dance
Focus on innovators of the early C20th e.g. Duncan, Fuller, Allan, Denishawn, Graham	Each one presents an insight and a wealth of material for further study
Valuable notes and bibliography	

invaluable as scholarly examples of an investigation into the works of a theatrical impresario and a choreographer respectively.

Sorell's translation and editing of the Wigman book combines both his own personal tribute to her work with her writings on dance.

All these examples are limited in time span by the life of the person and in geographical scope by their travels during that time or by the productions of their works across a number of countries and after their deaths.

3.2.1 Accounts of the life and work of notable figures in dance history

Title	Time span	Geographical range	Scope and major concerns	Sources used
Lynham, D. *The Chevalier Noverre. Father of modern ballet* London: Dance Books 1972	Noverre's life 1727–1810	W. Europe	An account of Noverre's life and work as theorist and choreographer within the context of the ballet of the time	Original contemporary sources carefully annotated Details 80 ballets, 24 operas, 11 small works
Buckle, R. *Diaghilev* London: Weidenfeld and Nicolson 1979	Diaghilev's life 1872–1929	Russia W. Europe	An account of Diaghilev's life and work, with the hindsight of 40 years	Meticulous detail matching interviews, newspaper reports, correspondence, articles, theatre programmes, manuscripts Annotated with precision
Macdonald, N. *Diaghilev observed by critics in England and the U.S. 1911–1929* London: Dance Books 1975	Diaghilev's USA and London visits 1911–29	England USA	The presentation of major review of the works of the Diaghilev companies over a 28-year time span	Contemporary first-hand accounts of of performances from the *Daily Mail*, *The Times*, *The Lady*, *Vogue*, etc. selected to present a range of views Original illustrations
Shelton, S. *Divine dancer. A biography of Ruth St Denis* N.Y.: Doubleday 1981	St Denis' life 1878–1968	USA	An examination of St Denis' aspirations and her work both personally and professionally	Use of many original newly discovered sources Indicates British sources that could be followed up

40

Structure and content	Evaluation
Chronological account of his life and work followed by an assessment of his contribution to the ballet Uses Noverre's own writings and descriptions of his ballets	Noverre's aesthetic and compositional theories outlined and placed in the context of prevailing ideas as well as his own productions
Appendices include translated scenarios; details of known productions, both first and later performances	A very readable introductory text based on a sound scholarly use of sources
Index subdivided by subjects, e.g. ballets, composers, librettists, etc.	
18 chapters arranged chronologically under general headings, e.g. 'The Early Years', 'The Movement West', 'The Fokine-Nijinsky' period	Relevant for any student of the life of an artist or animateur and as an example of detailed research and the balancing of sources of evidence
Accounts by and about collaborators from all artistic disciplines provide a vivid day-by-day view of his life and work	A very important resource book for the period and for the works and the artists involved
Press notices grouped chronologically in relation to first performances of works	Invaluable as a reference book for the choreography and subsequent perform-ances of Diaghilev's works
Changing reaction to particular dances can be monitored through time	Major works and critics represented
Information about the creation of the works provides the context for the reviews and links the sections	An excellent example of this type of study, a life through the eyes of the critics, and also as an account in its own right of the period
Long quotations used for the summary of his life and for accounts of earlier Russian performances	
A chronological account of Ruth St Denis' life and work in which the social and historical context from which she emerged is linked with the existing dance of the time	A useful critical biography which presents her life, her romances, motivations, etc., in conjunction with her work
Detailed descriptions of some of her dances provide a rare and qualitative account	Attempts to explain the origins of, and to characterise, her style, the stages of her choreographic and personal development
Her own dance concerns are related to those of other dancers of the period	
Detailed bibliography	

3.2.1 Accounts of the life and work of notable figures in dance history (*cont.*)

Title	Time span	Geographical range	Scope and major concerns	Sources used
Sorell, W. (ed., trans.) *The Mary Wigman Book* Conn.: Wesleyan U.P. 1973, 1975	Wigman's life 1886– 1973	Central Europe visits to USA	A translation and presentation of some of Wigman's writings as choreographer, theorist, dancer and poet	Her own writings, correspondence, poetry, views and reviews American response to her work Hanya Holm's first-hand account of Wigman's work compared with contemporary US work
Vaughan, D. *Frederick Ashton and his ballets* London: A. & C. Black 1977	Ashton's life since 1904	England, tours abroad	An account of the development of Ashton's choreography through over 80 ballets, films, musical and operatic works	Ashton's own writings and choreographic notes Newspaper and periodical reviews of his work. Letters, interviews. Critics, performers and choreographers' views all represented

3.2.2. *Collected writings of choreographers, performers and theorists*

The first two books in this section range widely through time. Both Cohen and Steinberg contain articles by performers and choreographers and, in addition, Steinberg includes contributions on the role and place of dance. Brown limits the scope of her text by the form of dance, that of modern dance, and hence, by definition, to the last years of the nineteenth century and to the twentieth century. The writings she presents are those of major choreographers.

Livet's text is also controlled by the form of dance that it covers.

Structure and content	Evaluation
Basically chronological but under titles of 1. Reminiscences of early work with Laban	Both a tribute to Wigman and a well-translated and researched presentation of her work, in its written form and in the memories of others
2. Statements on the dance	Her theories of composition, of form and process, the use of music, etc., are of value in a study of the historical development of theories of composition in the art of dance
3. American tours	
4 .Swastika years	
5. Post-war years	
6. Poetic and other writings	
Sorell's contribution in the first part and his own comments on her work	
Combines description and analysis of works with critics' comments in a chronological account of Ashton's life so far	Not a biography in the usual sense since it concentrates on the works and their structure and not his personal life
Structure of chapters relates to the amount of dance interest, i.e. one early chapter covers 22 years of his life while a later one covers a single year, 1934	Ashton's way of working, his methods and the craft he employs become evident A very valuable scholarly resource for work in this period of British Ballet as well as for the choreographer himself
Chronology Substantial bibliography subdivided Appendix comments on change in choreographic structure of *Les Rendezvous* over time	

The limit of the time span is twenty years and the form is that of post-modern dance, overlapping to some extent with Brown but giving more detailed attention to the later period. This allows comment not only from choreographers but also from critics, theorists, and other observers of the dance scene.

Banes, too, deals with the post-modern dance but in a different way. She lets the writings of the people themselves stand in their own right but also provides the historical and social context of the emergence of the new form through a series of essays about the works they have produced.

3.2.2 Collected writings of choreographers, performers and theorists

Title	Time span	Geographi-cal range	Scope and major concerns	Sources used
Cohen, S. (ed.) *Dance as a theatre art* London: Dance Books 1974, 1977	1581–1974	Europe USA	An anthology of primary sources, the writings of major choreographers, performers and theorists in the history of dance	Original technical manuals, statements of theory, discussion of performances. Some new English translations
Steinberg, C. (ed.) *The dance anthology* N.Y.: Plume 1980	1558–1978	Europe USA	Collection of essays by those involved in dance and in theorising about it, also provides a guide to the dance literature	Original primary sources, writings of dancers, etc. Essays on dance from first-hand observations and original theoretical discussion
Brown, J. (ed.) *The vision of modern dance* London: Dance Books 1980	C20th	USA	Presentation of the writings of important dancers and choreographers in the history of modern dance	Original primary sources, writings of these individuals
Livet, A. (ed.) *Contemporary dance* N.Y.: Abbeville 1978	1960–78	USA	Anthology of lectures, interviews and essays by and about choreographers, dancers, critics and scholars of dance	Original writings and photographs The latter capture historic moments both of the dance and design for it

Structure and content	Evaluation
Writings presented with brief intro-ductions from a wide historical period, from The Court Ballet e.g. Caroso C18th e.g. Weaver Romantic Era e.g. Bournonville Russia e.g. Petipa Modern dance e.g. Duncan Classical e.g. Balanchine Recent rebels e.g. Cunningham	Essential student source text of primary source material for theatre dance from the late C16th to mid C20th Relevant pithy introductions by this major American dance historian

Introduction to each of three sections draws historical threads together
1. Dance as a collaborative art
      e.g. Nijinsky, Benois
 	
2. Dance aesthetics and theory
      e.g. Denby, Langer, Martin
 	
3. History of dance from courts to modern dance e.g. Beaumont, Sorell, Crisp
 	
4. Selective chronology; family trees; guide to literature including notation guides and references to related arts
	Useful source text for essays about dance as movement; as drama; its links with design and music; its role in society and theories of art related to it
	
	Mixture of primary sources and essays

Arranged chronologically with four main sections 1. The forerunners, e.g. Duncan, Fuller, Wigman 2. The four pioneers, i.e. Graham, Humphrey, Weidman, Holm 3. The second generation, e.g. Cunning-ham, Limon, Nikolais, Hawkins 4. The new avant-garde, e.g. Halprin, Rainer, Brown, Dunn J. & D. 5. Bibliography sectioned under 'artists' and topics such as 'choreography', 'criticisms', etc	Very useful source text for modern dance and later developments. One of the most up-to-date collections of writings not otherwise easily available in this country Introductions to each section link the whole historically
Introduction places writings in the US historical context in the growth of the post-modern dance 1. Writings by e.g. Brown, Childs, Farber 2. Writings by critics, e.g. Jowitt, Kirby 3. Writings by historians, e.g. McDonagh 4. Highly detailed but selective chrono-logy 1902–78 of performances, par-ticularly detailed from the 1960s	Invaluable reference to dates and places of performances and collaborative works in the post-Cunningham period Major influences and developments since modern dance traced

3.2.2 Collected writings of choreographers, performers and theorists

Title	Time span	Geographi-cal range	Scope and major concerns	Sources used
Banes, S. *Terpsichore in sneakers* Boston: Houghton Mifflin 1980	1960–80	USA	A documentation of the emergence of a new form of dance through the writings those involved	Primary sources, writings of first-hand observers and those making the works

3.2.3 *Collected writings of dance critics*

These writings might be characterised as representing the immediate response of a critic to a dance, whether it is a new work or a different or later interpretation of an existing one. That moment of response is historically important. Later reaction by the same critic or reference to the reactions of other observers begins to demonstrate change in critical response through time. These differing responses are only possible with the progression of time and the consequent opportunity to see a work more than once.

The number of texts of this kind has increased markedly in recent years and many others of value could have been included. The most obvious omission is the writing of Marcia Siegel on the American modern dance.

3.3 *Companies*

3.3.1 *Histories of dance companies*

The historical framework of the texts on the Royal Ballet and the Ballet Rambert companies is limited simply by the years of their existence. Both provide factual material of value, the Royal Ballet account being particularly detailed, while the Ballet Rambert text is more of a personal tribute to Marie Rambert.

The chronology and factual basis provide historical documents which in themselves are primary written source material. For the use of company archival material in the history of dance see Chapter 5.

46

Structure and content	Evaluation
Writings of major post-modern dance figures placed in detailed socio-historical perspective. Traces trends, general areas of agreement, etc. between such people as Brown, Halprin, Rainer, Monk, Dunn, King	Illuminating attempt to give insight into the most recent developments in dance without imposing standards of judgement derived from earlier styles. Very useful

3.3.2. *Guides to the current repertoire, works placed in historical context*

These guides to the repertoire provide a historically relevant account of dances in that they pinpoint moments in history when certain dances were choreographed and/or were most frequently performed. These cumulative moments make up the history of dance. As works of reference they are basic to any investigation into a particular dance or a choreographer, designer, composer or dancer. They may also be useful in giving details of specific performances.

While the factual details provide a useful starting point, these texts should be treated with caution since they tend to assume an interpretation based on a simple story-like account.

3.4 *Contemporary literature*

3.4.1. *Historical accounts of the dance in the literature of a period*

These texts have in common an analysis of the dance as presented in literary works written in the relevant periods. The kind of analysis involved is a stage removed from considering the dance itself or first-hand accounts of it. The dance may be regarded as a literary image, and the differing images of dance through time may inform us about the place and perceived importance of the dance and its power as a metaphor for other spiritual or worldly ideas.

47

3.2.3 Collected writings of dance critics

Title	Time span	Geographical range	Scope and major concerns	Sources used
Coton, A. V. *Writings on dance 1938–1968* London: Dance Books 1975	1938–68	Europe USA	To analyse the critic's function and to present 30 years of reviews of dance from Jooss to classical ballet and Graham works	Author's reviews for the *Daily Telegraph* 1954–68 and other publications from 1938 First-hand critical accounts of performances and discussion of new trends
Denby, E. *Looking at the dance* N.Y.: Horizon 1949, 1968	1930s–40s	USA	Collected reviews of performances of modern ballet and modern dance	Author's reviews for *N.Y. Herald Tribune, Dance Index, Dance Magazine*, etc., written in the 1930s and 40s.
Buckle, R. *Buckle at the ballet* London: Dance Books 1980	1940–75	Europe USA	A historic collection of selections from Buckle's critical output	Author's reviews mainly for the *Sunday Times*, some date back to the 1940s First-hand critical accounts
Croce, A. *Afterimages* London: A. & C. Black 1978	1966–77	USA	Collected reviews of Croce's work	Author's first-hand accounts written for *Ballet Review, The New Yorker, Dancing Times* and others.
Jowitt, D. *Dance beat. Selected views and reviews 1967–76* N.Y.: Dekker 1977	1967–76	USA	Critical reviews of dance performances selected to demonstrate 'the liveliness and variety of the N.Y. dance scene'	Author's reviews for *Village Voice, N.Y. Times, Art in America, Dance Calendar*, etc. First-hand accounts with later additions on further viewings

Structure and content	Evaluation
1. Comments on the critic's function 2. Reviews from the 1943 and 1945 seasons, then 1961 3. Reviews under headings of 'English ballet'; 'Foreign ballet'; 'Modern dance', grouped together 4. Chapter on 'What's the use of critics?'	One of the few critics to state clearly what their role might be and to argue for an objective, historically located method of criticism Focus on principles and themes Excellent example of critical writing and of change of views through time
Reviews grouped under headings such as 'Meaning in ballet'; 'Ballets in recent repertoire'; 'Dancers in performance'; 'Notable events'; 'Ballet music and decoration'; 'Modern dancers'; 'Dancers in exotic styles'	Points to the critic's function as animating perception, ranges widely in discussion Very valuable first-hand accounts by this major American dance critic of the early period, including reconstructions of Duncan's works
Chronological sections deal with 1. America 1959–60 2. Russia 1961–62 3. Royal Ballet 1963–65 4. Classics 1966–68 5. Western Europe 1969–71 6. New trends in Britain 1972–75 with additional reviews from other periods	Humorous, perceptive portrayal of many facets mainly of the ballet world, although some accounts of Graham and British modern dance Excellent reference work for criticisms of the period [1]
Different types of writing for different publications clear from the division of the text into 1. weekly articles 1973–77 2. monthly articles 1969–71 3. quarterly essays 1966–72 4. occasional pieces Ranges from classical ballet to the post-modern dance	Very informative collection of writings recording well-argued views of contemporary performances Very good reference work for US performances, an example of reaction to works through time and in relation to emerging genres
Preface on the role of the critic and use of language; her own preconceptions Sections divide into: ballets, mostly new; 'Sunday' pieces; modern dance, pioneers and 2nd generation; 3rd generation, mostly rebels; ancient festivals; reports on revivals of early modern dance works	Delightfully descriptive collection of reviews, accepting a wide range of activity under the heading of 'dance' Open style captures the fleeting moment Very good reference work for US performances and for the appraisal of works over several viewings

3.3.1. Histories of dance companies

Title	Time span	Geographical range	Scope and major concerns	Sources used
Bland, A. *The Royal Ballet. The first fifty years* London: Threshold 1981	1931–81	Britain tours abroad	A comprehensive history of the growth of a major classical ballet company, the Royal Ballet	Statistics and other factual material from the archives of the Royal Ballet, not otherwise generally available
Crisp, C., Sainsbury, A., Williams, P. (eds.) *Ballet Rambert 50 years and on* London: Scolar 1976, rev. 1981	1926–81	Britain	A history of 55 years of the Ballet Rambert and a tribute to its founder	Personal accounts of those closely involved with the company through its time span

Structure and content	Evaluation
Chronological account of the growth of the company, its policies and practice over 50 years to its establishment as a national company	An essential reference work for any study of a choreographer, the works or different performances connected with the Royal Ballet company
Highlights changes in direction and new developments, e.g. in touring and in the school	Provides a very valuable starting point for many further studies
Statistics section contains the repertoire productions and itinerary of the R.B. and S.W.R.B.: dancers, choreographers and works made for the company: casts for different performances: films and T.V. performances	Otherwise an eulogy and personal tribute to this national institution
Chronological account pinpointing crucial moments in the history of the company from the viewpoint of those involved	The many short contributions span the lifetime of the company and range from dancers and choreographers to stage staff and directors
Introduction by Osbert Sitwell, contributions from Mary Clarke on the first 40 years and from the following, plus others: Ashton, Markova, Tudor, Van Praagh, Gore, Gilmour, Tetley, Chesworth, Morrice, Williams	Very useful to any student of the company and its repertoire and of a choreographer or dancer who worked with the Rambert company
Chronology of repertoire 1926–81. Lists of artists and other staff	

3.3.2 Guides to the current repertoire, works placed in historical context

Title	Time span	Geographi-cal range	Scope and major concerns	Sources used
Balanchine, G. Mason, F. *Balanchine's festival of ballet* N.Y.: Doubleday 1954, 1978	C19th and C20th	Europe USA	Description of 404 major classical and contemporary ballets	Programme descriptions, critics writings assembled also from other secondary sources
Clarke, M. Crisp, C. *The ballet goer's guide* London: Joseph 1981	C19th and C20th	Europe USA	A guide to 100 classical and contemporary ballets performed frequently	Secondary background sources, with the authors' own critical reviews assembled
Brinson, P. & Crisp, C. *A guide to the repertory. Ballet and Dance* Devon: David & Charles 1980	C19th and C20th	Europe USA	A guide to over 130 works currently available from the classical and modern dance repertoire	Secondary sources plus critics' first-hand accounts
McDonagh, D. *The complete guide to modern dance* N.Y.: Doubleday 1976	1880–1970	USA	A historical account of modern dance through descriptions of 225 of the works of over 100 choreographers	Original sources not always checked against other primary evidence Some inaccuracies in performance dates

Structure and content	Evaluation
1. Scene by scene account of ballets of the past and present which are 'of lasting importance', accompanied by the comments of critics, composers and choreographers Listed in alphabetical order by title 2. Series of short essays on how to enjoy ballet, Balanchine's life, and a brief history of dance 3. Extended chronology of significant events in the history of dance	A good starting point for details of dances and their first performances Recommended for beginners with care over the interpretation placed on the dances needed
1. Background to ballet, brief history and section on making dances 2. Stories of the ballet, selected as major works in the repertoires of the Royal Ballet, Ballet Rambert, American Ballet Theatre and the Nederlands Dance Company Arranged by title, in alphabetical order 3. Brief sections on the dance steps, the dancers and the choreographers	Basic reference work for details of dances and some different productions of the same dance although not definitive in this respect Describing the dances as 'stories' emphasises literal meaning and creates difficulties with more abstract works
1. Brief background to the history of ballet 2. Dances divided by the era to which they belong with Introductions to each section. Under headings of 'Romantic ballet'; 'Imperial Russian ballet'; 'Diaghilev'; 'British classical ballet'; 'British modern dance'; 'Americans and Europeans, and the future' Descriptions in terms of stories and some qualitative evaluation 3. Further study and reading list	Provides a historical perspective on the repertoire Useful as an introduction to dances before seeing them for the first time and as an outline of facts for a study of a specific dance or a choreographer and her/his repertoire
1. Basic information given about the life and work of choreographers selected, with a description of some of their dances and a chronology of their works. Uses critical reviews as comment 2. Divides the period into The Forerunners, e.g. Duncan; The Founders, e.g. Graham; In and out of the Steps of the Founders, e.g. Tetley; Freedom and Formalism, e.g. Nikolais, Charlip, Brown, Childs 3. Chronology of significant events, lists of journals and further reading	First major choreochronicle of modern dance Good basic source for an introduction, but facts should be checked against further evidence since new information has now emerged Information on collaborations, times of first performances, etc., useful 'Choreographic families' helpful in an introduction to modern dance

3.4.1. Historical accounts of the dance in the literature of a period

Title	Time span	Geographical range	Scope and major concerns	Sources used
Brissenden, A. *Shakespeare and the Dance* London: Macmillan 1981	Shakespeare's life 1564–1616	England	Literary analysis of the dance as found in his plays, as imagery and as a representation of contemporary practice	The plays, notably: *Love's Labour's Lost* *A Midsummer Night's Dream* *Much Ado About Nothing* *Romeo and Juliet* *Macbeth* *Timon of Athens* *Pericles* *Henry VIII* Manuscripts, contemporary dance writings
Priddin, D. *The art of the dance in French literature* London: A. & C. Black 1952	Early 1800s–1930s	France	An examination of the stance of critics and poets towards the dance	The writings of Gautier, Mallarmé, Lemaitre, Gheon *et al*, Valéry, in the form of essays and criticism

Looking at existing dance history texts in this way is a starting point in an important process. This process is one of moving from accepting the words written on a printed page as representing some kind of absolute truth, to being critically aware that dance history consists of balancing available evidence and piecing together an interpretation of the sources in an attempt to arrive at an explanation of dance events that can be justified.

Ultimately, the professional dance historian does this on original material which no other person has used in the same way. The texts described in this chapter are examples of some of the better works

Structure and content	Evaluation
Two general chapters on 1. Dance and the Elizabethans. Describes the social context and political events, the ritual and social dances of the time 2. The history plays and the imagery of dance Then deals in turn with the Comedies, the Tragedies and the last plays, relating the dance and dialogue; characters and plot; the dance as ironic visual symbol; the dance as cosmic imagery	Argues that the different types of his plays can be distinguished as much by the changing use of dance imagery as by themes and characters Very useful for combined arts courses, English/Drama students as well as dance students with literary interests
Chapter 1 isolates recurring themes in the dance writings presented, e.g. the relation between dance and the other arts particularly music Subsequent chapters characterise Gautier's quest for beauty; Mallarmé's notion of dance as abstract and metaphorical; Lemaitre's predictions of a Diaghilev-style collaboration; Gheon and others' reviews of the early Diaghilev seasons; Valéry's ideas on pure motion related to those of the philosopher Bergson	A specialist text that requires considerable background and understanding of both dance and French thought General themes, however, are of wide interest historically since they are seen to recur in different guises, despite differing aesthetic ideas

from the dance history literature. A comparison of these with some other texts should make it abundantly clear that much dance history writing is superficial and unverified, and that there is work to be done to raise the standard of historical writing about dance.

It is in the nature of the historical study of dance that it is never fixed and undisputed. The appearance of new evidence, the development of techniques of analysis and further study of possible interpretations will always allow for increasingly refined evaluations of events in the history of dance.

References

Backman, E. L. 1952, 1972 *Religious dances in the Christian Church and in popular medicine*. Conn.: Greenwood

Balanchine, G. & Mason, F. 1954, 1978 *Balanchine's festival of ballet*. New York: Doubleday

Banes, S. 1980 *Terpsichore in Sneakers*. Boston: Houghton Mifflin

Bland, A. 1981 *The Royal Ballet. The first fifty years*. London: Threshold

Brinson, P. & Crisp, C. 1980 *A guide to the repertory. Ballet and Dance*. Devon: David & Charles

Brissenden, A. 1981 *Shakespeare and the Dance*. London: Macmillan

Brown, J. (ed.) 1980 *The vision of modern dance*. London: Dance Books

Buckle, R. 1979 *Diaghilev*. London: Weidenfeld & Nicolson

Buckle, R. 1980 *Buckle at the ballet*. London: Dance Books

Clarke, M. & Crisp, C. 1981 *The ballet goer's guide*. London: Joseph

Cohen, S. (ed.) 1974, 1977 *Dance as a theatre art*. London: Dance Books

Coton, A. V. 1975 *Writings on dance 1938–68*. London: Dance Books

Crisp, C., Sainsbury, A., Williams, P. (eds.) 1976, rev. 1981 *Ballet Rambert 50 years and on*. London: Scolar

Croce, A. 1978 *Afterimages*. London: A. & C. Black

Denby, E. 1949, 1968 *Looking at the dance*. New York: Horizon

Emery, L. 1972 *Black dance in the U.S. from 1619–1970*. Cal.: National

Gautier, T. 1932 *The Romantic Ballet* as seen by Théophile Gautier, trans. from French by C. W. Beaumont. London: Beaumont

Guest, I. 1966 *The Romantic Ballet in Paris*. London: Pitman

Hilton, W. 1981 *Dance of court and theatre. The French Noble style 1690–1725*. London: Dance Books

Jowitt, D. 1977 *Dance beat. Selected views and reviews. 1967–76*. New York: Dekker

Kendall, E. 1979 *Where she danced*. New York: Knopf

Kirstein, L. 1935, 1942, 1969 *A short history of classic theatrical dancing*. New York: Dance Horizons

Kraus, R. 1969 *History of the dance in art and education*. New Jersey: Prentice Hall

Lawler, L. 1964 *The dance in Ancient Greece*. Conn.: Wesleyan U.P.

Livet, A. (ed.) 1978 *Contemporary dance*. New York: Abbeville

Lynham, D. 1972 *The Chevalier Noverre. Father of modern ballet*. London: Dance Books

Macdonald, N. 1975 *Diaghilev observed by critics in England and the U.S. 1911–29*. London: Dance Books

Magriel, P. (ed.) 1948, 1978 *Chronicles of American Dance from the Shakers to Martha Graham*. New York: Da Capo

McDonagh, D. 1976 *The complete guide to modern dance*. New York: Doubleday

Priddin, D. 1952 *The art of the dance in French literature*. London: A. & C. Black

Quirey, B. 1976 *May I have the pleasure?* London: B.B.C.

Ranger, T. O. 1975 *Dance and society in Eastern Africa 1890–1970*. London: Heinemann

Richardson, P. 1960 *The social dances of the C19th in England*. London: Jenkins

Rust, F. 1969 *Dance in society*. London: Routledge & Kegan Paul

Ruyter, N. L. 1979 *Reformers and Visionaries: The Americanisation of the art of dance.* New York: Dance Horizons

Sachs, C. 1933, trans. 1937 *World history of the dance.* New York: Norton

Shelton, S. 1981 *Divine dancer. A biography of Ruth St Denis.* New York: Doubleday

Sorell, W. (ed., trans.) 1973, 1975 *The Mary Wigman Book.* Conn.: Wesleyan U.P.

Sorell, W. 1981 *Dance in its time.* New York: Doubleday

Stearns, M. & J. 1964 *Jazz dance. The story of American vernacular dance.* London: Macmillan

Steinberg, C. (ed.) 1980 *The dance anthology.* New York: Plume

Vaughan, D. 1977 *Frederick Ashton and his ballets.* London: A. & C. Black

PART II

Approaches to historical study based on different kinds of dance sources

The purpose of these three chapters is to demonstrate the range of materials available in journals and periodicals, in dance company archives and in a town or region of the country. The nature and range of sources available differs in each case although there is some overlap – for example, between Chapter 4 and Chapter 6, dealing with journals and periodicals and a town or region which may, of course, produce and/or hold such materials itself. However, once the sources have been located, then analysis of them for what they reveal of dance can start. The approaches which are described in each chapter are examples of how such vast possibilities can be reduced to manageable proportions through selecting themes; e.g. short periods in time, particular styles of dance, individuals who were important at different times such as choreographers, performers, theorists.

The sense that the historian can make of the past is dependent very largely on the kind of materials and evidence that exist, hence the importance of using them in a valid and reliable manner.

CHAPTER 4

Newspapers and dance periodicals with particular reference to British publications

by Judith A. Chapman

4.1 The location of information
4.2 Newspapers and dance periodicals as a resource
4.3 Types of information to be found in newspapers and periodicals
4.4 Summary of ideas for projects using newspapers and/or periodicals

Newspapers and dance periodicals are documents of the utmost importance for purposes of historical study since their contents are for the most part primary source materials (as defined in Chapter 2). Collections of newspapers and/or dance periodicals built up through the years in school, college or local public libraries provide a treasure house of information for an infinite number of projects in the history of dance.

This chapter identifies different kinds of information which are to be found in newspapers and/or periodicals and outlines a selection of historical projects which might result from using them. The searching out and analysis of such resources, together with the interpretation of findings in relation to other events of the period, provide an exciting and accessible approach to the historical study of dance. Newspapers and periodicals offer up-to-date information about events, performances, people, companies and views about dance. Such publications might be termed 'history-in-the-making' and are a starting point for investigating the past and for studying factors which have contributed to the contemporary situation. They provide information about the period in which they were written and thus enable the student to make contact with different aspects of the period.

4.1 The location of information

In practical terms, when deciding on a topic for a study using newspapers and periodicals, the student needs to find out what is available in local libraries. Sometimes both national and regional newspapers are held on microfilm. Occasionally, a library will possess collections of periodicals such as the *Dancing Times*, *Ballet* or the *Journal of the English Folk Dance and Song Society*. The National Resource Centre for Dance (University of Surrey) is in the process of locating substantial holdings of dance periodicals in both institutions of education and public libraries. A local newspaper office may hold a range of reference materals – for example, bibliographies and indexes – and perhaps a unique collection of reports and photographs of local scenes and events which may provide insight into dance and into the social life of the community during a particular period.

In order to search out information from newspapers, the student would be well advised to become acquainted with a number of 'finding aids' such as *Handlist of English and Welsh Newspapers 1620–1920* which explains when papers began, ended or merged. Some newspapers have existed for quite short periods of time whereas others continue publication for many years. The existence of a newspaper today is no guarantee that it was in existence during the period selected for study. Similar information is contained in the *British Union catalogue of periodicals*. The annual *Press Guide* compiled by Willing provides details of newspapers still in existence.

Most newspapers are not indexed and so it is necessary to search through many issues and pages, though if a single event such as a performance can be accurately dated then it is more easily found. For *The Times* there is Palmer's Index running from 1790 to 1941 and the Official Index which started in 1907. The Official Index lists names, places and subjects. This Index is available in many large public libraries as well as the British Museum Newspaper Library at Colindale which is also the British repository for all post-1800 London as well as provincial and foreign papers. More recently, an Index to *The Financial Times* has been compiled.

4.2 *Newspapers and dance periodicals as a resource*

When using either newspapers or periodicals as a dance source it becomes important to be able to recognise the characteristic features of any publication and to be familiar with the background and bias of the person writing, who may be either a critic, reviewer or general journalist.

The writer in one newspaper or periodical may assume that the reader has quite considerable knowledge of dance whilst another writer will assume little. In the first case the writer may provide detailed analysis of the structure and content of the dance, and an interpretation of the performance seen, as well as reference to other dances by the same choreographer, to other works in the repertory of the company and/or to further interpretations of the same dance. A writer assuming little knowledge in the reader may merely provide information about the company, dancers, choreographer, the background and training, with a less detailed analysis of the dance itself.

As well as identifying in general terms the kind of readers towards whom the writing is directed there is, of course, the need to establish the background and experience of the writer and this provides further insight into the stance taken in the writing. What is the critic's understanding of dance? Is the critic's experience of only one, or of many kinds of dance? Is she/he solely a dance critic? Does the critic also write about the theatre in general? Is the music critic who writes about dance drawing on a knowledge of music to do so? Quite evidently there must be some attempt to identify factors such as these before the value and bias of the criticism can be assessed.

Newspapers

Newspapers are intended for the fast transmission of the latest news and views upon events. Nationally circulated newspapers issued each weekday morning provide the means whereby a critic can publish a review of a performance of the previous evening. Later editions of the same morning or evening newspaper may carry different reviews reflecting the time that the paper 'went to press'.

The demands of writing within the time constraints imposed by the need to meet the deadline for publication of the next morning's newspaper must inevitably result in certain problems for the critic. The dance may have only been seen performed on one occasion and, particularly in the case of a new work or even an unfamiliar dance style, it may be difficult to appraise after one viewing and in such a short time. In addition, when a review must be written for a deadline there is little time to ponder over the choice of words, metaphor or even to search out background information about the work (though this may, of course, have been part of the critic's preparation before seeing the performance). Thus writing about a performance in this immediate manner must, of necessity, demand rather different skills from the review that is written for a Sunday newspaper or periodical. In the latter case the critic has more time to reflect on the work and to select the words with which to appraise it. The critic may have opportunity to see the dance in more than one performance, possibly with a different cast, and may see the dancers and the company in other programmes. This leads to the conclusion that reviews written without the constraints of the deadline for a daily newspaper tend to be rather more substantial and considered than those written with such restrictions.

Dance periodicals

The periodicals referred to here have been selected for their coverage of dance in the theatre, education and the community. Dance periodicals have certain characteristics, and it is useful to identify briefly some features of selected British periodicals. Of the monthly publications the *Dancing Times* is the longest established, the first edition having been published in January 1910 in London. (There is an earlier publication called *Dancing Times* which appeared from 1894–1909, but this is not easily accessible.) During its early years of publication the *Dancing Times* contained articles on social dance, theatre dance, private dance schools and dance education. It is now concerned mainly with dance as a theatre art with perhaps more substantial coverage of classical ballet than contemporary dance.

Another London monthly is *Dance and Dancers* which started publication in January 1950. It ceased publication in September 1980 and resumed in October 1981. *Dance and Dancers* has, throughout its existence, contained articles of both national and international interest on theatre dance. In recent years the contents have given considerable coverage of contemporary dance. For example, in December 1981 and January 1982 *Dance and Dancers* contained reviews of Britain's third Dance Umbrella season, which took place in the autumn of 1981, and also brief articles examining the value and achievements of what was described as 'an international festival of contemporary dance'.

A bi-monthly periodical entitled *Ballet* was published and edited by Richard Buckle from July/August 1939. After Vol. 1. No. 2. no more were published until January 1946 because of World War II. In October 1948 the title became *Ballet and Opera*, changing again to *Ballet* in January 1950. *Ballet* ceased publication in 1952. For its brief span of existence this periodical provided a fascinating glimpse into ballet with articles by choreographers, dancers, film makers, critics and teachers.

Ballet Annual was first published in 1947 with the stated objective of making 'a special feature of archive material so valuable for reference in the future' (Ballet Annual No 1, p. 2). It contains chronologies of ballet in England and abroad, general critical articles, historical writings and contributions by musicians, designers and dance educators. Volumes 1–14 of *Ballet Annual* were edited by Arnold Haskell, and Volumes 15–18 by Arnold Haskell and Mary Clarke (currently editor of the *Dancing Times*). *Ballet Annual* ceased publication with Volume 18 in 1964.

Two periodicals launched more recently are *New Dance* and *Impulse*. *New Dance* is a quarterly first published in New Year 1977. It was conceived by the members of X6 Collective who decided to give a voice to artists working in the growing community of 'alternative' dance activity in the United Kingdom, that is dance which exists largely outside the conventional theatrical setting. It provides a platform for the exchange of ideas about 'new dance' activities, lists classes and events and vigorously reviews dance performances.

Impulse (not to be confused with the now defunct American dance annual of the same name) is the bi-annual publication of the Inner London Dance Teachers' Association. It provides information about performances, courses and other events, articles of topical interest to dance educators and occasionally articles by children.

Another periodical published by an association is *Movement and Dance: Magazine of the Laban Guild*. This has been published bi-annually since 1947, initially as a Newsletter, later titled *Movement* and then, until the first issue in 1982, as the *Laban Art of Movement Guild Magazine*. This periodical is concerned primarily with the work of Rudolf Laban, dance in education and topics related to these two. It is a source of information about the development of dance teaching in the maintained sector of education in the United Kingdom and its articles, letters, reviews and information about courses and conferences provide insight for the student of dance history into changes and areas of topical concern in dance education.

The *Journal of the English Folk Dance and Song Society*, published three or four times each year since September 1936, provides a wealth of information about the traditional dance, music and customs of the United Kingdom. This is the specialist journal of the Society which has its headquarters at Cecil Sharp House in London. The contents include coverage of festivals and other events which involve dance, notices of courses and conferences, details of selected dances and their accompaniment, advertisements and numerous photographs. It provides a fascinating record of attempts to keep alive some of the fast disappearing facets of the British heritage. The *Folk Music Journal*, published annually since 1965, provides academic articles, reviews and reports of research into a range of topics associated with the traditional dances of the United Kingdom.

The most recent publication, which includes both dance and drama, is *2D*, first published in Autumn 1981 and promoted by Leicestershire Education Committee and County Drama Workshop. Its stated aim is to support the development of dance and drama by providing a forum for the exchange of ideas and information. The intention is to cover the whole area of dance and drama in education and to publish 'material by individuals who are pushing forward the boundaries of our practice and our thinking in Drama and Dance'. In addition, it is stated editorial policy to offer material which provides guidance for the teacher.

4.3 *Types of information to be found in newspapers and periodicals*

In general both newspapers and periodicals provide a platform for the communication of ideas and of current information. Their more or less regular, and usually frequent, publication enables information contained within them to be more up-to-date than is possible with a book. In order to identify the different kinds of information contained in newspapers and periodicals, the two will be discussed together since there is obviously much overlap and some distinctions in relation to purpose have already been identified.

Both periodicals and newspapers may be searched for:

— calendars of events

— criticisms or reviews of performances and descriptions of folk dance festivals

— feature articles containing historical background to dances and/or festivals, information about companies, choreographers, dancers

— advertisements relating to classes, courses and training, clothing for dance and book reviews.

Such witting and unwitting testimony (see page 21 for definition) may contribute invaluable insights into events, artistic and social attitudes and understanding of the customs and stylistic conventions of the period in which they were written.

A *calendar of forthcoming events* is often sited near the beginning of a periodical and is a useful tool in several ways. In a current periodical it informs the reader of what is available in the coming weeks, and, in the historical sense, it is a means of finding when and where a company performed, as well as details of works in the repertory of that time. Thus, if a student is tracing the work of a particular company or choreographer, or examining changes in the repertory of a company, or requires information about the visits of foreign companies to theatres in the United Kingdom, a calendar of events is a valuable tool.

In addition a calendar of events gives an indication of trends through time and the changing types of events and festivals taking place. For example, the 8th news sheet published by the Laban Art of Movement Guild in March 1952 gives information on two forthcoming courses: one to be held in London and directed by Rudolf Laban and Lisa Ullman, the other to be held at Dartington Hall. Information such as this might be traced through time in a periodical or periodicals, thus building up a picture of the types of courses available for dance teachers. With additional information, such as a list of course members, or a reference found elsewhere to a specific person attending the course, it would be possible to ascertain that particular individuals were in the same place during the same period of time, thus indicating that there existed opportunity for exchanging ideas either intentionally or incidentally.

Alternatively, a calendar of events might be the basis of a factual comparison of dance performances available to audiences in the United Kingdom in the year 1979 as compared with 1969. This gathering of information and analysis of what was available for theatre goers would provide interesting results in terms not only of, for example, the number of small contemporary dance companies which had come into being by 1979, but also of the extent of change in the repertoires of the larger, established classical ballet companies

Criticisms or *reviews* about dance performances provide invaluable information both about the performance and also about the attitude and bias of critics at any point in time.

Analysis of criticisms and reviews in a selected newspaper or periodical will show which dances were in the repertoire of companies reviewed and also, when compared with the calendar of events, which companies and dances the critic chose to write about. Criticisms or reviews from a specific period will also reveal particular attitudes and understanding of that period – either the stance of the critic selected or the more generally accepted attitudes of the time, or both. In analysing a work the critic may refer to the conventions of the particular style of dance. For example, in a dance in the classical genre reference may be made to established structures of classical works or particular aspects of the classical technique, as these had evolved at that point in time, and in relation to standards and expectations which the critic has, and expects readers to have. Thus, criticisms or reviews in either newspapers or periodicals may provide information about certain attitudes at the time they were written which are evident in the writings of one or more critics and which may be traced through time in order to analyse changes.

Reviews may also provide information from which changes in the performance and/or staging of a dance may be noted. It will, of course, be the case that each critic chooses to report on different aspects of the dance, but through careful analysis of one critic's writing perhaps about a première, subsequent performances and even revivals or reconstructions, it is possible to extract points which are significant historically. For example, John Percival in writing about the new Peter Wright and Philip Prowse version of *Swan Lake* for Sadler's Wells Royal Ballet draws attention to the more 'Russian accent' than in earlier Royal Ballet stagings and suggests that the general style 'is gothic as seen through Russian eyes in Tchaikovsky's time' (*Dance and Dancers*, January 1982, pp. 10–12). He notes also a change in both the music and choreographic structure of the new *Swan Lake*. In Act IV the orchestrated Tchaikovsky piano pieces which were added for the 1895 Petipa and Ivanov production are omitted; instead Wright, as others have done, uses music from Act III for a Seigfried and Odette tragic duet.

Reviews about folk or ethnic dance performances or festivals may appear in specialist periodicals, in newspapers or in periodicals where the chief concern is with other dance genres. It is necessary to remember when reading these three distinct types of publication that the writers will be writing for rather different kinds of reader in each instance. Again the background that the reviewer brings to bear in any attempt to transmit to the reader understanding of the dances of other peoples and countries is of significance. References may be made to the place of dance in its social context, therefore offering insight into both the dance and the historical and artistic culture in which it exists. Information may also be given about music, steps and formations and their manner of performance in a dance, and changes from one part of the country to another and/or from one date of performance to another may be noted.

Some periodicals contain *feature articles* about dancers, companies, critics, dancers, dances, or topics which are currently of general interest. Such articles are of relevance to the student of history not only because of the information contained within them but also because of the particular subjects chosen for the feature article at any point in time. Presumably, whatever the subject of the feature article, it was considered to be of topical interest when written. Thus from 1954 onwards, following the first visits of American modern dancers such as Martha Graham and Doris Humphrey to the United Kingdom, there are in both *Dance and Dancers* and the *Dancing Times* a number of articles which attempt with varying degrees of perceptiveness to assess this 'new phenomenon'. An analysis of such articles and their content through time would provide an interesting basis for a project in dance history. Any article will, of course, reflect both the bias of its author and the context of the time when it was written. Thus an article about the 1954 and 1963 visits of the Martha Graham Company to the United Kingdom written in the late 1970s will differ from one written in the mid 1960s in having the advantage of hindsight, and perhaps would contain very different insights into those early performances.

Advertisements in both newspapers and periodicals form a further source of material for study and provide much valuable information about the period of publication. Advertisements cover a wide range of topics, from information about classes, courses and training establishments, to clothing, shoes and job vacancies. For example, it is possible to trace from advertisements in both *Dance and Dancers* and the *Dancing Times* the year in which a college of higher education first advertised an undergraduate degree course in dance or one which combined dance with one or more other subjects. Advertisements may provide evidence for the existence of certain styles of dance in that a performance is mentioned, or a course or school of dance teaching the specific style is publicised. Thus, a date may be established as a starting point for further investigation. For example, the *Dancing Times* in 1935 contains an advertisement for the Anny Fligg School of Dance in London which offers classes in the Laban technique, this providing one fragment of evidence of work existing in this country based on Laban's Central European dance prior to World War II.

A *correspondence section* is a regular and important feature of virtually all periodicals and newspapers. Its particular interest lies in the fact that it is the only part of the publication to which readers contribute directly. Such columns are an open platform for letters which may promote discussion, exert considerable influence over developments in dance, and also provide a forum for debate and protest in relation to matters of current concern. All such letters enable both the editors and the readership to be in contact with some of the viewpoints of national and/or regional debate. The letter written by Fokine and published in *The Times* on 6 July 1914 provides an example of correspondence which proposed radical innovations and which, as a result of the wide audience that it reached, generated much discussion about classical ballet. The five principles which Fokine summarised in his now historic letter outlined fundamental ideas for the reform of classical ballet. These had first been formulated in the production notes which accompanied a scenario for a ballet which Fokine sent to the Russian director, Teliakovsky, of the Imperial Theatre in 1904, on the eve of the February revolution. His proposals had little effect during this period in Russia and Fokine's choice of *The Times* for the later publication of his five principles perhaps shows his total refusal to compromise for reasons of expediency and his desire to generate change and gain influence.

Photographs in newspapers and periodicals form a further visual source of material for study. They may illustrate points made in articles or reviews and provide evidence of the style of a dance. Some problems in the interpretation of visual material such as photographs are referred to in Chapter 2.

4.4 *Summary of ideas for projects using newspapers and/or periodicals*

The kinds of historical studies which might result from using newspapers and dance periodicals as source materials are numerous.

This type of source material provides a rich fund of information about the era in which it was written and one or more periodicals from a selected time span can provide the basis for a study of that period. These may be the main source, e.g. the *Dancing Times* 1920–25, or may be supplemented by reference to other sources – visual, audio, book materials or other periodical and newspaper sources of the time. Reference to, and analysis of, the general content of a newspaper of the period chosen for study brings the student into immediate contact with the period. World events which were happening concurrently, together with information about everyday occurrences, social gatherings, festivals and festivities, performances in theatres taking place in London and provincial towns at the same time all contribute towards a greater understanding of that time as a whole.

A method of categorising different types of investigation is suggested in Chapter 11. All four categories of investigation might be carried out using only newspapers and/or periodicals as source material. Topics which might especially draw on these kinds of source materials are summarised as follows:

1. Investigations in relation to young *artists* and *groups of artists*, e.g. young choreographers, dancers, newly formed companies.
2. Investigations in relation to particular *dances*.
3. Investigations in relation to *dance criticism*, e.g. attitudes of a specific time are implicit in the writings of critics.
4. Investigations which are *thematic*. These are topics which are currently of interest and about which discussion has occurred at different times in the past, e.g. theories of dance technique, the funding for dance and dance groups.

A project on young choreographers, recently formed companies or new works can only be carried out by drawing on a substantial proportion of source materials from newspapers and periodicals of the time. Current happenings necessitate a contemporary account of events. For example, at the present time little historical study has been carried out to trace the beginnings and subsequent development of contemporary dance in the United Kingdom, or to identify and analyse factors contributing to this. Materials, written and visual, are scattered though much could be drawn together from newspaper and periodical sources.

Within this general period, a project might focus on a particular choreographer, dancer or company and consider influences on the development and trends in work. If a choreographer, such as

Richard Alston or Robert North, is selected, the project might examine his work through considerations of:

— the traditions from which he emerged and the attitudes of society of the time to dance,
— the artistic climate of the time, e.g. contemporary arts movements and artistic conventions,
— the characteristic features of his work, e.g. selection of movement in relation to the idea, choreographic form, use of set design, costume, sound accompaniment, performance space,
— contemporary reviews and writings, and reviews written over a period of time.

Projects concerned with a selected dance work might be based on the notion that certain themes have been used by artists and choreographers as a source of inspiration in music, drama, the visual arts and dance. For example, a biblical theme such as 'The Prodigal Son' has been used by choreographers working in different historical periods and dance styles; similarly Shakespeare's *A Midsummer Night's Dream* has been the source of ideas for ballets by Ashton (1964), Balanchine (1962) and de Warren (1981) to name but three. A project of this kind would begin from the identification of different choreographic interpretations of the theme selected, and would involve an analysis of the artistic and social context from which each version selected for study emerged. Newspapers and periodicals would be used to search out reviews of performances in years when dances were choreographed and first performed and also with regard to later performances. Thus, the characteristic features of a particular treatment of the subject matter might be analysed with reference to source materials.

Attitudes to dance can be examined through analysis of the dance criticism of a period. For example, a student may undertake an analysis of the contents of *Dance and Dancers* in specified years, or a comparative study of two years in order to analyse, interpret and critically discuss the information collected. This kind of study would quite obviously demand that the student have a sound knowledge of developments in dance in order that information collected and analysed could be understood and interpreted in context.

Quotations from *The Sunday Times* and *The Observer* in 1954 serve to illustrate the attitude of two critics writing about the first visit of the Martha Graham Dance Company to London. Cyril Beaumont, dance critic for *The Sunday Times*, wrote (7 March 1954):

71

Miss Graham's dance form, inspired like her sets by ultra modern art, is a complete negation of normal conceptions. Arm and leg positions are deliberately distorted. Steps often begin with the working foot (toe upward) thrust forward, and there is much use of staccato pelvic tilts, constricted thorax and abdomen and rolling on the floor. There is little continuity, no flow and often one phrase of movement appears unrelated to the rest.

This critic, typical of many writing in the United Kingdom at this time, reveals in the last sentence something of his expectations – that 'continuity', 'flow' and 'related phrases of movement' are necessary elements in a dance. Richard Buckle, writing on the same date in *The Observer*, stated:

Now I conjure every idle habit-formed fellow, in need of a third eye to see more beauty, that he should visit the Saville Theatre and watch Martha Graham. She is one of the great creators of our time . . . I hope all thoughtful people will see her, for she has enlarged the language of the soul.

In 1954 reviews of Graham's work were short, often on the back pages or tucked away in a corner and difficult to find, which again is an indication of the stance taken not only by the critics but by the newspaper editors.

The final category suggested – that of an investigation which is thematic – is self-explanatory and requires no further examples.

It is evident that the varied contents of newspapers and periodicals constitute a most valuable resource for a historical study of dance. In pursuing a study based on these sources the following points need consideration.

1. The availability of source materials would have to be established and a selection made according to the objectives of the area defined for study.
2. The background and stance of the critic and the potential audience would need to be identified.
3. Knowledge from the other columns of a newspaper about events which were occurring simultaneously would provide a broader artistic, social, political, economic and religious context in which to understand the dance.

72

4. Knowledge of what happened before and after the period isolated for study would be necessary in order to clarify the extent of the period and how it could best be defined.

It is perhaps the contact with the *actual period of the dance* and the information that was written *at the time* which contribute most to making newspapers and periodicals such an exciting resource for dance history.

CHAPTER 5

Dance company archival material with particular reference to London Festival Ballet

by Joan W. White

5.1 The nature and range of dance company archival material
5.2 The dance company archive – its use, actual and potential
5.3 Procedures for using a company archive
5.4 Examples of studies in dance history using company archival material

The dance company is a living source. The concern here is with the raw data of the dance, both human and material. Here is history in the making. As such then dance company archival material is of fundamental importance to the serious student of dance history. In this chapter the importance is illustrated by:

5.1 examining the nature and range of dance company archival material;

5.2 explaining how the collation and ordering of such material determines the actual and potential use of the archives;

5.3 suggesting procedures for the effective usage of the company archive;

5.4 discussing examples of studies in dance history, using company archival material.

5.1 *The nature and range of dance company archival material*

The dance company archive is a very specific source. Except in rare instances it is concerned exclusively with the company to which it is attached and consists predominantly of primary source material. Material may be categorised in a variety of ways, as described in Chapter 2. In order to facilitate discussion in this chapter, the broad categories suggested in Chapter 2 have been adopted and these have been further subdivided to give some indication of the more specific range and nature of materials available for study. This categorisation appears in diagrammatic form on page 76. It is important to note that categories are not mutually exclusive.

Indicated in the diagram is the major distinction between the first-hand, contemporary, raw material generated by the dance company, i.e. *primary source* material, and the second-hand interpretation or reportage, derived from the primary material, that is the *secondary source*. For purposes of clarity *primary* sources have been subdivided into visual, written and aural categories.

Visual primary source materials have been further categorised according to their association with *publicity, performance* or *performance retention*. Many of the visual materials, in a company archive – for example videos, tapes or films – though of obvious importance to an art as ephemeral as dance, are of recent origin. Numerous problems arise when attempts are made to collate, retain, preserve and store visual sources. Techniques involved are often sophisticated demanding up-to-date, expensive apparatus such as video cassette recorders and television cameras, and these are frequently beyond the means of most companies. Even preserving costumes which at first may seem simple is, on examination, very complex. Should all costumes be preserved? If not, how many? Whose? What are the criteria for selection? Frequently by the time a work is out of the repertoire costumes are well-worn, making preservation more difficult. A wardrobe supervisor with a limited budget will frequently be on the look out for materials which can be used again. Assuming it were possible to preserve all costumes, sets, etc., the space required to house the visual materials associated with a major work such as *The Sleeping Beauty* would make the operation prohibitive. The effect of all this on the student of dance history is that visual sources are both scarce and fragmentary causing difficulties in relation to interpretation, reliability, authenticity and value.

Problems associated with the interpretation of photographic materials have been discussed in Chapter 2, but such material, originally devised for publicity purposes, is frequently retained in company archives because it presents few immediate storage problems and often photographs are the only means of studying a work no longer in the repertoire. The distinction in respect of sets, costumes and properties between the actual objects in each case, and designs and models made beforehand is of importance in itself. In addition, photographs may reveal a change which had to be made, usually by the choreographer, from the first thoughts of an

DANCE COMPANY ARCHIVAL MATERIAL

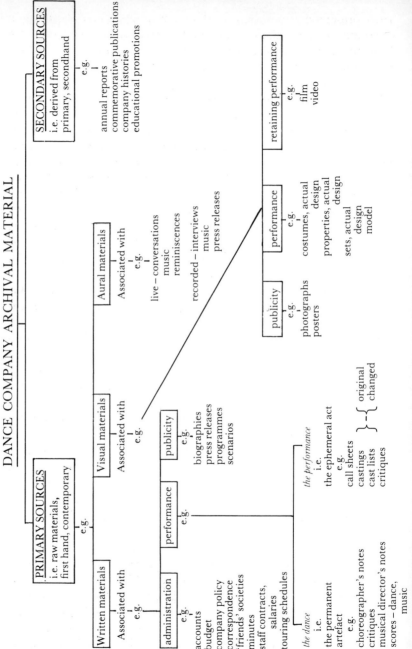

PRIMARY SOURCES
i.e. raw materials,
first hand, contemporary

e.g.

Written materials
Associated with

e.g.

administration
e.g.
accounts
budget
company policy
correspondence
'friends' societies
minutes
staff contracts,
salaries
touring schedules

performance
e.g.

the dance
i.e.
the permanent
artefact
e.g.
choreographer's notes
critiques
musical director's notes
scores – dance,
music

the performance
i.e.
the ephemeral act
e.g.
call sheets
castings   ─ ╲
cast lists   ┤ { original
critiques   ─ ╱   changed

publicity
e.g.
biographies
press releases
programmes
scenarios

Visual materials
Associated with

e.g.

publicity
e.g.
photographs
posters

performance
e.g.
costumes, actual
             design
properties, actual
             design
sets, actual
         design
         model

retaining performance
e.g.
film
video

Aural materials
Associated with

e.g.

live – conversations
music
reminiscences

recorded – interviews
music
press releases

SECONDARY SOURCES
i.e. derived from
primary, secondhand

e.g.

annual reports
commemorative publications
company histories
educational promotions

artist presented in a design, to the realisation of these thoughts in performance. For example, in London Festival Ballet's *Romeo and Juliet* the designer Ezio Frigerio made a large boat for Act I but the choreographer Nureyev decided that he wanted more space, so the boat appeared at the first stage call only and by the time of the dress rehearsal it had disappeared completely and now exists only in photographs. Important, too, is the need to be aware of the distinction between the kind of film or video produced as a direct record of a production, likely to have been viewed from the front with minimal or no changes of camera angle, and the 'presentation' film or video where the director arguably is acting in the role of 'second choreographer'. Here selection for the camera, in the form of close-ups, focusing on certain dancers and alternative camera angles, means that the dance as presented to the audience has changed. A case which exemplifies this point nicely is Robert Cohan's *Stabat Mater* as given in the theatre and Bob Lockyer's interpretation of the work for B.B.C. television. Without doubt, however, films and video-tapes are invaluable records. They are our only means of capturing and preserving the performance of great dance artists of both the present and the past. Nevertheless, it must be remembered that the film or video-tape records only one interpretation of a choreographer's work. Other interpretations may be equally valid.

Written sources form the largest part of the dance company archive. For purposes of clarity these may be sub-categorised into written sources associated with *administration, performance* and *publicity*. Again it is important to note that lists are not definitive, nor categories mutually exclusive.

Much of the material categorised as administrative is, as might be expected, concerned with the everyday running of the company and needs little elaboration. Activities of societies attached to companies such as the Friends of Covent Garden, London Festival Ballet, Northern Ballet Theatre, Scottish Ballet, the Place Society, are slightly different, though most often closely associated with company activity. Their relevance to the dance company archive varies. The societies' activities in many instances are administered by a secretary whose salary is the responsibility of society funding. Permanent staffing of this kind ensures that activities are promoted by and recorded for society members but indirectly benefit the company as a whole. Events such as works in progress, open rehearsals and lecture demonstrations, using the human resources of the company, are often made accessible through 'Friends' activities. On some occasions, as was recently the case on 2 July 1981 when artistic director John Field worked with two couples from London Festival Ballet on the Act II pas de deux from *Swan Lake*, the whole evening was video recorded and will now form part of a permanent visual record in the company archives. Written records of the societies' activities are kept and in certain instances publications result. These range from *About the House*, an extensive magazine of the Friends of Covent Garden produced three times a year, to more informal newsletters such as those produced by the Friends of London Festival Ballet.

Written materials associated with performance may be classified in such a way that the dance, i.e. the permanent artefact, is distinguished from what has here been described as the 'ephemeral' or 'single' performance. Materials exemplified in the category of the dance are self-explanatory though perhaps it is important to draw attention to the fact that it is still not common practice for all major companies to have the services of a notator, hence dance scores are not available for some works in the repertoires of major companies. The problem is of even greater concern for small companies. In the category of the dance performance a distinction has been made between original castings, i.e. the cast on whom the work was choreographed or reconstructed and cast lists, i.e. subsequent castings for seasons. In respect of cast lists and call sheets it is important to distinguish further between the original list and any changes. Such changes are often made without prior notice; without a good archivist or archive-conscious companies, these changes may go unrecorded and thus the reliability of information is in doubt (c.f. Chapter 2).

Aural, like visual source material, has benefited from developments in technology. Dances have always been handed down aurally and visually – i.e. one generation of performers will teach the next – but the potential for recording such teachings is a comparatively recent development. However, sound recording is now a relatively simple, inexpensive operation and this has led to an increase in aural source materials. The amount and range of sound material on the radio alone is vast. It is expected in the more obvious arts programmes such as 'Kaleidoscope' or 'Critics Forum' but coinciding with the so-called 'dance boom' of the last decade, programmes such as 'Woman's Hour' and 'Today' frequently present informed interviews. Additionally, useful information about dance personalities can be gleaned from programmes such as 'Desert Island Discs'. In a recent programme on 2.May 1981, Sir Frederick Ashton was featured and revealed much concerning his tastes in music and the early influence of people and places on his development as choreographer, performer and director. Often a company archive may hold sound copies of such interviews.

Of great value to the dance historian are face-to-face conversations with an artist. In the past these have been lost since they have gone unrecorded. More recently these situations have been exploited. Companies often organise events, sometimes for the Friends, other societies, or in conjunction with performances both in the capital and in the regions, where, for example, choreographers talk about their works, dancers talk about their interpretations of a role, designers talk about their intentions and the extent to which they have been realised or modified, or artistic directors talk about their policies. This is valuable historical material in the making. Fortunately companies are realising increasingly the importance of such events and, for example, in the case of London Festival Ballet who promote many such activities, these are now almost all recorded where possible and copies of the sound and video-tapes are held in the company archive.

While some company archives house a wide range of secondary source material ranging from well known reference books and texts to dance periodicals, the sources which are of concern in this chapter are those which are specifically associated with the company to which the archive is attached. Examples are company histories, commemorative publications, educational promotions and annual reports. They are derived almost exclusively from the primary sources of the company archive.

Company histories such as Mary Clarke's *Sadler's Wells Ballet – a history and an appreciation* are published at various intervals throughout a main company's existence. Commemorative publications too are usually historical in nature, the distinction being that they are produced to coincide with specific milestones in a company's development. The year 1981 marked the fiftieth anniversary of The Royal Ballet and there has been a proliferation of commemorative publications, perhaps the most significant of which is Alexander Bland's *The Royal Ballet: the first 50 years*. Ballet Rambert celebrated their fiftieth anniversary, London Festival Ballet their twenty-fifth and Scottish Ballet their tenth with *50 Years of Ballet Rambert* edited by Clement Crisp, Anya Sainsbury and Peter Williams, *London Festival Ballet 1950–1975* by Peter Williams, and *A Ballet for Scotland: The first ten years of Scottish Ballet* by Noel Goodwin, respectively. The major ballet companies, for example Royal, Sadler's Wells, London Festival and Scottish also publish year books which are extensive documents, well presented, often lavishly illustrated and giving details of the current company personnel and repertoire.

An increasing number of 'educational' publications are produced by the companies. Usually these are in the form of kits or packs on works in the company repertoire such as London Festival Ballet's *Swan Lake* and *Romeo and Juliet*, and the Royal Ballet's *La Fille Mal Gardée* and *Swan Lake*; guides to viewing performances such as Ballet Rambert's *Dance Appreciation Teaching Units for Schools and Colleges*; and more general publications such as Ballet Rambert's *Ballet Rambert on Tour* and Sadler's Wells Royal Ballet's *Curtain Up*. All of these publications are written with young audiences in mind and are often designed to be used in conjunction with the human resources of the company.

Company histories and commemorative and annual publications are largely descriptive and are the writer's interpretation of the primary sources usually held in the company archive. The educational material, whilst having a very specific function, is often largely descriptive but attempts to focus attention on specific aspects of dances or company life and work through questions, illustrations and game-like activities such as crosswords, puzzles, cut outs, etc. Since all of these publications are secondary sources, often with a declared purpose in mind, the student of dance history has to be aware of possible bias.

5.2   *The dance company archive – its use, actual and potential*

It is suggested that the main functions of a dance company archive are *conservation, promotion, reconstruction, reference* and *study*. Potential users range from members of the company itself to critics, those working in television or radio, dance writers and historians and serious students and teachers of dance. Company archival material is automatically generated. No matter how small or temporary a company, whether it be a single dancer or a group, their existence as performers will mean that the raw data of an archive – programmes, costumes, designs, press releases, dances, etc., will come into being. However, material automatically generated does not constitute an archive. This will require action on the materials, action which will determine both the character of the archive and how it is to be used.

The dance company archive is unique and one of its main values is that it locates the company in time and place. Its distinctive character is automatically determined by the company, the materials it generates, how those materials are ordered and where the archive is located. For the larger companies materials are housed at the company headquarters. For example, Ballet Rambert in Chiswick, London Festival Ballet at Festival Ballet House, South Kensington, Northern Ballet Theatre at Manchester, Scottish Ballet in Glasgow and Royal and Sadler's Wells Royal at the Royal Opera House, Covent Garden. Smaller companies with no permanent base usually carry all materials with them or they are temporarily housed with members of that company. Clearly, there are major storage problems and much material is lost in this way. The problems of smaller companies are discussed later in this section.

The nature and range of a dance company's archival material has been described previously and is shown diagrammatically on page 76. How such material is ordered is dependent on many factors and determines the extent of its usage, both actual and potential. A key figure in this is the company archivist, who is responsible for servicing the archive.

The company archivist is a rare being in the dance world. Information indicates that currently John Travis of London Festival Ballet and Jane Pritchard of London Festival Ballet and Ballet Rambert are the only archivists exclusively concerned with dance. John Travis' appointment in 1975 as archivist with London Festival Ballet is on a part-time basis, the remainder of his employment being with the company's education and community unit. Jane Pritchard initially worked with London Festival Ballet voluntarily. She was appointed as archivist to the company on a part-time basis in January 1982, working two days a week. In June 1982 she was appointed to Ballet Rambert on a part-time, three days a week basis, hence she is the first full-time dance archivist, though her services are shared between two companies.

There has long been an archivist associated with the Royal Opera House at Covent Garden, whose responsibilities have embraced both The Royal Ballet and Sadler's Wells Royal Ballet but have also been concerned with The Opera. For this reason the archivist here might be more accurately described as a theatre archivist having responsibility for the activities within the theatre as a whole rather than specifically in relation to dance. Numerous theatres have an archivist but these, being general appointments, are outside the scope of this chapter. Northern Ballet Theatre is of particular interest since their archive has been built and maintained by a succession of archivists in training. These people were seconded to the company, on a part-time basis, from Manchester University, where from 1978–81 the University ran a one-year Diploma Course in Performance Arts and Theatre Collection Studies. Both the archivists at London Festival Ballet, Ballet Rambert and at the Royal Opera House hold this award. The suspension of this course in 1981 raises serious questions as to the future training of archivists.

It is through the services of the archivist that material is *collated, ordered* and made *accessible*. The archivist determines what is to be collated, the number of copies of each item to be held and how best they may be preserved and maintained. A difficulty here is actually getting hold of the material prior to its disposal by someone who genuinely thinks of it as having little value. One of the responsibilities of the archivist, in this respect, is to make all members of the company *archive conscious*. For example, the company archivist is unlikely to tour with the company, so the help of company members, very often the dancers themselves, has to be enlisted to collect call sheets, cast lists, etc. Once these have been collated, there are as many techniques for maintaining and preserving sources as there are sources themselves. Information on the maintenance and preservation of source material, whilst of major importance, is a subject of study in its own right and outside the scope of this text.

How material is ordered is also of major importance. Currently this is a chance affair. Companies without a permanent archivist, yet who are conscious of the need to retain their sources, tend to store them with the minimum of ordering. A company archivist usually devises or inherits a system of ordering. The diagram on page 76 might well form a basis of such a system. The ordering of archival materials affects its accessibility and ultimately determines its usage.

For materials to be accessible an archive has to be open. Currently no dance archives are open to the extent of, for example, a library –

even a specialist library. The London Festival Ballet archive is in an ordered form and its materials are widely used, but the archivist cannot permit general accessibility and cannot publish regular opening hours. All queries are dealt with in an informed manner and the archivists are most generous in giving their time, but this does not constitute general accessibility. Additionally, accessibility demands facilities for usage, such as a room out of the way of general company business, to permit users to study materials. In most instances spaces at company headquarters are over-used already and study space for a company archive may well be low on the list of priorities. An archive can only be open if it is staffed, which calls for an informed person to find relevant materials, advise on their use and answer any questions as well as requiring continuity of ongoing collating and ordering. This is without doubt a full-time job and, depending on the size of the company, would occupy more than one person.

The current position appears bleak since with so many limitations the actual use of a dance company archive is severely restricted. The increasingly difficult financial position of most companies is unlikely to ease this situation. Companies most often have other priorities: dancing, choreographing, building audiences, touring and trying to maintain and extend a repertoire on a very meagre budget. Not all companies are achive conscious, hence much valuable material is lost. Even where a company is aware of the value of their resources these remain inaccessible if no one is responsible for collating and ordering such materials. Where materials are available and ordered, lack of adequate staffing means that their usage is curtailed and the range of persons having access is consequently limited.

Yet despite all this the dance company archive, consisting as it does of sources which are almost exclusively primary ones and hence extremely valuable, is fundamental to historical study. This study might be of the company itself, of all artists who are or have been involved with the company directly or indirectly, and of the development of that company within the specific dance form, or more widely within the development of dance in Britain. The *potential* use of the company archive then is vast and some consideration as to how that potential may be realised might be useful here.

Recommendation 8 of the Gulbenkian Report, *Dance Education and Training in Britain* (1980), states:

Archives. Dance institutions in both sectors should recognise the importance of dance archives for education and training purposes, and their own responsibility for safeguarding the material under their control. A conference should be called as soon as possible to concert and discuss the preservation and use of dance archives in Britain, and appropriate appeals to funding bodies. (p. 174)

The dance section of the National Association for Teachers in Further and Higher Education organised such a conference in March 1981. In October 1981 the University of Surrey appointed a Director to establish the National Resource Centre for Dance which is sited on the university campus at Guildford. Additionally, the past decade has seen the initiation of degree studies in dance, both single and combined honours. Coupled with this are the expanding examination opportunities for dance at C.S.E., C.E.E. and G.C.E. 'O' and 'A' level. Currently discussions are taking place for the inclusion of dance in the proposed new system of examining at 16+. All of these developments have increased demand for resources. This has meant that companies are constantly being asked for materials. Such demands have led to companies being increasingly archive conscious, but they have also highlighted at least two major problems: first, the necessity for some kind of planning so that the potential use of the company archival material may be realised and second the need to identify how best to use the archive once it is organised (see Section 5.3).

Clear plans will need to be formulated to deal with the first problem and all parties involved would need to be consulted, but it seems that the current situation could set a possible framework. The National Resource Centre for Dance at the University of Surrey is planned to become the computerised 'nerve centre' for a nationwide network of resource centres. The archival material of the major companies, which locates the company in place and time, would seem to be most appropriately housed at that company's headquarters. Here it is readily available for everyday use by company members but may be made sufficiently accessible for more general public useage. An agreed national cataloguing system would ensure that each company could have a computer link with the National Resource Centre. Eventually questions concerning usage from the general public might go via the National Resource Centre and thus companies would not be troubled by people who require access to materials which are not unique to that company archive. This would not obviate the need for a company archivist nor would it solve the problem of space for a study and viewing area for potential users, but it would be likely to make the archivist's task more manageable. Smaller companies without a home base could, if they wished, house their source material either at the National Resource Centre itself or at a suitable regional centre which may be a theatre, university, college, local library, arts centre, etc. Hence materials would be ordered and accessible and problems of loss and storage overcome. Such a network, it is suggested, would ensure that the potential use of a company's archives is fully realised.

5.3 *Procedures for using a company archive*

A company archive is not a general library. It is a unique, highly specialised, valuable primary source for the study of dance. It is suggested that this should be borne in mind by the potential user. Too often company archivists and education officers tell tales of letters that are received asking for all the information on, for example, The Royal Ballet, 'requesting an interview with the company director' for a C.S.E. project, or asking about a choreographer and spelling his name incorrectly. Such requests indicate ill-informed use and should never reach the companies.

The potential range of users is vast. In the majority of instances such users are themselves specialists, aware of the problems of using source material and sensitive to the priorities and working life of the company. Requests of the kind identified above usually come from young users and it is with these that this section is most directly concerned. This is particularly important since all the major companies have education officers who are extremely anxious to complement the teacher's role in providing young people with an education in dance.

The discussion above of the nature and range of dance company archival material includes educational promotions. These secondary sources are very often linked with the primary human resources of the company. Here the education officer draws on the archive material or, in London Festival Ballet's case, works with the archivist to ensure an appropriate learning experience for the young people concerned. Activities on offer by most companies include lecture demonstrations, matinees, backstage theatre tours, talking to dancers, watching make-up and lighting effects, etc. The list of activities is endless and it seems the goodwill of the companies, in this respect, is boundless. It may well be that this is the root of the problem since often so much goodwill on one side can induce reticence or, worse still, complacency on the other. The final responsibility for the education of young people, whether at school or college level, rests with the teacher. As such it is the teacher's job to plan an ongoing programme of dance education – which may or may not lead to an examination in the case of older pupils or students – and to identify the resources needed to ensure the fulfilment of that programme. Once this has occurred, an approach to the company education officer and the resultant dialogue between education officer and teacher will clarify aims and objectives and will ensure the most effective learning experience.

Procedures such as these apply not only to taking advantage of the activities that companies offer but also to written requests for information. Ill-informed requests of the kind exemplified would not occur if teachers accepted their responsibilities in respect of the company archive. For example, the C.S.E. candidate whose examination requires the writing of a project would have had considerable tutorial help from the teacher. Consequently the project title would be a manageable, specific area. The teacher would have advised on ways of approaching the study and the pupil would have completed some general reading from school or local library books, periodicals, programmes. It is only when the pupil is sufficiently informed to ask the appropriate questions of the archivist or company education officer that the company resources should be used. They can then be an intelligent source of study. In the majority of instances it is appropriate that the teacher should contact the company.

London Festival Ballet's advisory educator's group is currently writing *Guidelines for using a Dance Company as a Resource for Education*, and a publication such as this will no doubt clarify the problems and reassure the educators.

5.4 *Examples of studies in dance history using company archival material*

Two limitations govern examples of studies described in this chapter. The first is that they are historical in nature, in other words they will be concerned with *change through time*, since this is the subject of the book. The second is that they must be limited to possibilities *which use a company archive* — in other words, the concern is with the kind of studies in dance history that are truly dependent on dance company archival material.

Even with these limitations the range of possibilities is vast. For this reason an attempt has been made to classify potential study areas, to describe these generally, present them diagrammatically and then to select 4 models for more detailed discussion.

The diagram on page 88 illustrates how potential study areas might be categorised according to the company, individual personalities and dances. Inevitably there is overlap and the lists are by no means definitive. Examples of studies in the 'company' category might look at policy, finance or significant dates in a company's development. Studies such as examinations of how sponsorship affects the repertoire over a period of time or how company policy implicitly and explicitly affects the activities of the education team might form topics for students in tertiary education. Studies involving the kinds of personalities identified on page 88 might range from straightforward accounts of who they are, when they joined the company, what they do, etc., to a sophisticated analysis of, for example, the contribution of a choreographer, dancer, composer, designer, etc., to the ongoing development of the company or a comparative evaluation of the policies of two artistic directors. Focus on dances might lead to studies of works in progress, how the same works have changed through time in terms of choreography and performance, analysis of changes in style, or a straightforward account of what is currently in the repertoire and how this has changed over the last five years. All of these categories are relevant for any major topics such as a general history of the company over a specific period or an examination of artistic developments and an evaluation of the way in which these might reflect trends in the development of dance in Britain. The point to remember here is that a company archive is the source material for the study of a company and those who are or have been associated with the company over a period of time. This information forms the bank of knowledge in respect of a specific company. It is how that knowledge and information is used that changes according to the aims and objectives of those involved (see Chapter 10).

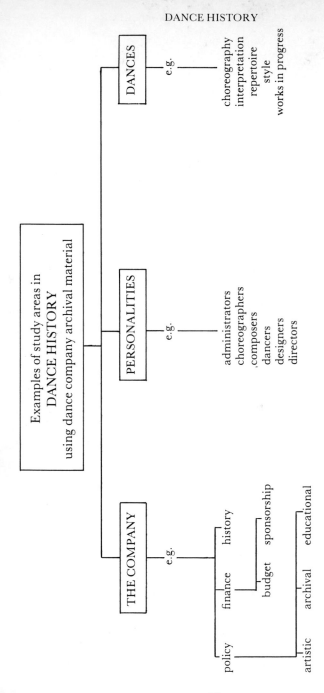

Examples of study areas in
DANCE HISTORY
using dance company archival material

THE COMPANY

e.g.

policy
finance
history
budget
sponsorship
artistic
archival
educational

PERSONALITIES

e.g.

administrators
choreographers
composers
dancers
designers
directors

DANCES

e.g.

choreography
interpretation
repertoire
style
works in progress

FOUR MODELS FOR STUDY USING LONDON FESTIVAL BALLET ARCHIVE

PROPOSED STUDY AREA	STUDY LEVEL	[SOURCES USED]	PRESENTATION
1. An examination of the contribution of Léonide Massine to the development of dance in the U.K.	Undergraduate	Primary visual: performance; props., sets, publicity materials written: performance; critiques, dance and music scores publicity: press releases, programmes, scenarios — Secondary annual reports commemorative publications	Report i.e. study approximately 10,000 words
2. Describe the development of London Festival Ballet from its origins to the present day. Include reference to the work of directors, choreographers and designers (N.B. This question could be directed to *either* directors *or* choreographers *or* designers)	G.C.E. 'O' level	written: performance; critiques, publicity; biographies, press releases, programmes — annual reports commemorative publications	Essay/examination question N.B. The actual question is taken from the specimen exam. paper for history of dance for the G.C.E. 'O' Level Mode 2 Dance. University of London, Schools Examinations Dept.
3. London Festival Ballet's seasons at the London Coliseum and the Royal Festival Hall 1975–80 (c.f. Leeds, Manchester, Bristol, Oxford)	C.S.E.	Visual: posters written: publicity; programmes, press releases, scenarios — commemorative publications educational promotions	Project
4. *The Sleeping Beauty*	Upper primary, 9–11 years	visual: costumes, photographs, sets, slides written: programmes — educational promotions	Class project involving drawing, models, painting, audio-tapes, descriptive writing

89

Four models for dance history students using dance company archival material
The four models are shown diagrammatically on page 89. Column
one indicates the topic area, column two the suggested level of study,
column three the company archive material to be used and column
four, a possible means of presenting the study for assessment
purposes should this be required. It should be noted that these are
suggested models only. Studies similar to those outlined have been
carried out with the age group concerned. In each of the models
the company archive used is that of London Festival Ballet for
the following reasons. Firstly, this is the archive with which the
author is most familiar and secondly, the archivist has agreed
that access to resources would be available for the kinds of models
exemplified.

Model 1 would clearly draw on material from other company
archives as well as that of London Festival Ballet but the *kinds* of
material would be similar. At this level it is suggested that a student
would approach the study area by reading a wide variety of
secondary sources, likely to be found in a college or university
library, and by viewing Massine's works where they are being
performed in a company repertoire and/or shown on film. Having
acquired general information the student would then approach the
company archivist. In this way the student would be able to discuss
the topic area intelligently with the archivist to determine the range
of source material that would further inform the study. A student of
dance history should be capable of selecting, analysing, interpreting
and evaluating primary source material appropriately. The whole
exercise would develop over a period of, for example, two terms and
would be interspersed with regular tutorial help from the dance
history tutor. The outcome should be an informed study which is
based largely on primary sources.

Model 2 is clearly on a much more restricted area. It is likely that it
would arise from a taught course situation. In this instance it is
suggested that the teacher would obtain copies of the secondary
sources of the archive such as *London Festival Ballet 1950–1980* and any
relevant reports. These are available from the company and would
be a useful addition to a school library. Furthermore, the teacher
might consult the archivist in order to be able to examine some of the
primary source materials to support the teaching of the course. A
visit to see London Festival Ballet when the company is performing
locally would also make the whole exercise more meaningful. The

outcome would be a short, descriptive essay the structure for which would probably best arise from help in a class discussion situation.

Model 3 is likely to be a collation of evidence but will also involve the C.S.E. candidate in searching out appropriate details. The area is quite specific and the time span manageable. It would be of particular interest if the pupil had had a continuous dance course in the secondary school from first to fifth year and, as part of that, had attended performances of the company at the theatres identified. The teacher or pupil may well have kept programmes or posters and the school library may have back copies of dance periodicals. Once again the teacher could obtain the relevant secondary sources from the company and could visit the archive to consult primary sources and advise the pupil through tutorials. C.S.E. projects are usually chosen by the pupil in the fourth year, so that the candidate would be able to view the company over a period of up to eighteen months. This requires planning but would be a way of keeping the ongoing study alive. The outcome would be a project, largely descriptive, with relevant illustrative material.

Model 4 is designed for the upper primary school age group an it is suggested that the children should focus on a specific work. Ideally this should be a dance that is currently in the company repertoire and likely to be performed at a theatre that they might attend. The whole exercise is likely to be teacher-directed though children would no doubt work individually or in small groups, each feeding their information into a total class project. The teacher needs to discover the works in the current company repertoire and the company's touring schedule. This information is readily available from companies up to a year in advance. The teacher then needs to consult with the education officer and the company archivist with requests for materials and a projected plan for the class to go to a performance. In the model on page 89 the work selected for study is *The Sleeping Beauty*. London Festival Ballet has an educational pack on this work and so the activities here might form part of the project.

Additionally, the teacher might use slides or photographs of, for example, costumes from different productions of *The Sleeping Beauty*. These could be used in a 'Spot the difference' game for the children. Differences identified would lead to discussions arising from questions such as: What are the differences? Why have they occurred? Who was responsible? Is the dance likely to have changed because of this? A similar exercise can be carried out with pictures, slides or models of sets. A pointe shoe can again lead to questions such as: What is it? Who wears it? Which characters in *Sleeping Beauty* wear them? Do dancers always wear such shoes? When did they start wearing them? Why? In both of these series of questions the children's attention has been focused on the change through time. In other words, they are automatically involved in dance history in a very tangible way. These class-based activities may be complemented with a visit by the children to Festival Ballet House where teacher and education officer can pool their knowledge and make the *Sleeping Beauty* even more meaningful. This might involve the children in seeing dancers on pointe, in costume, and experiencing for themselves how make-up and lighting effects are used to create characters. Ultimately, the children would see the actual performance in the theatre. The likely outcome of such a study might be a class project involving illustrative materials such as drawings, models, paintings; audio tapes made by the children simulating interview situations; descriptive writing, etc. The possibilities of presentation with this age group are limited only by the imagination of the children and the facilities they have to display and present their work.

In the discussion of the models it has been suggested that in three of the four examples the archive is used by the teacher rather than the pupil. The company archive is a highly specialised, unique source. It contains much perishable and irreplaceable material. Access to the archive is essential but such access should be for informed users, sensitive to the importance and value of the materials held. In the majority of instances dance history studies at school level can be adequately serviced using secondary sources. These secondary sources, i.e. the histories, commemorative publications, annual reports and educational promotions, are usually readily available for purchase from the companies. Additionally, visual materials are often given away. Students following dance history courses as part of their degree studies, who are knowledgeable about primary and secondary sources and who are informed in the techniques of the historian, might well be ready to use the archive themselves. In other words the company archive is best used by knowledgeable people who can specify their aims, discuss intelligently their needs with the archivist and are thus able to select, analyse and interpret their source materials effectively.

References

Bland, A. 1981 *The Royal Ballet: the first 50 years*. London: Threshold Books
Clarke, M. 1955 *Sadler's Wells: a history and an appreciation*. London: A. & C. Black
Crisp, C., Sainsbury, A. & Williams, P. (eds.) 1976 *50 years of Ballet Rambert*. Ilkley: Scolar Press
Goodwin, N. 1979 *A ballet for Scotland. The first ten years of Scottish Ballet*. Edinburgh: Canongate
Gulbenkian Foundation 1980 *Dance education and training in Britain*. London: Calouste Gulbenkian Foundation
Williams, P. 1975 *London Festival Ballet 1950–1975*. London: London Festival Ballet Trust

Additional Sources

Ballet Rambert materials for education:
    Ballet Rambert on tour
    Dance appreciation teaching units for schools and colleges

London Festival Ballet materials for education:
    Romeo and Juliet
    Swan Lake
    Guidelines for using a dance company as a resource for education (in preparation)

The Royal Ballet and Sadler's Wells Royal Ballet materials for education:
    Curtain Up
    La Fille Mal Gardée
    Swan Lake

CHAPTER 6

Regional evidence for dance with particular reference to a Yorkshire spa town, Harrogate

by Patricia A. Mitchinson

6.1 Locating source material
6.2 Harrogate sources
6.3 Other regional sources relating to Harrogate
6.4 Regional source material on Harrogate
6.5 Secondary source material
6.6 Primary source material
6.7 Harrogate histories

A *regional locality* can refer to any area or district delineated for the purposes of the study. It would, for example, encompass a whole or parts of a city, a town, or village. A locality might, therefore, be identified for its *urban* or *rural* characteristics although inevitably there will be points of overlap.

There may be a number of possible reasons for identifying a specific locality for a dance history study. The distinctive character of a particular city, town or village could be a significant factor in determining the *nature* of the historical study. Special features may exist such as buildings of particular dance interest: the local city Dance Hall or Palais de Dance, the spa town Assembly Rooms, each provide examples of landmarks in the history of dance and as such provide possible sources for investigation. The existence of other dancing places such as village maypoles or local 'dancing stones' may provide additional clues to the *context* in which the dance activity arose, e.g. social or ritualistic, and the *type* of dance activity which took place there.

A significant example of a building providing a clue to an aspect of dance history exists in the city of Norwich where a local cinema carries the name 'Noverre'. To anyone unfamiliar with the history of dance this name may well be meaningless, but to someone more knowledgeable it will be associated with the celebrated Jean-Georges Noverre (1727–1810). Further enquiries would then reveal the fact that this same Noverre was related to a well-known family of Norwich dancing masters and this could provide the basis for a possible area of study (see Fawcett Papers 1970).

Other approaches to identifying regional localities may lead to entirely different kinds of dance history studies. It could be interesting, for example, to select a locality at random and by referring to the indigenous source material subsequently discover *what*, if any, dance activities currently exist. This could be described as a 'here and now' historical study based on present-day dance events. Similarly, a locality might be identified in the knowledge that some form of dance activity *does* exist – e.g. a group of Morris or Sword Dancers – and by using this as a starting point subsequently discover more about its historical background. Such examples are to be found in cities where distinctive pockets of dance may have been formed by local community groups. It may be possible, therefore, to understand something of the sub-cultural traditions of a particular ethnic group in a city suburb without ever having set foot in its country of origin. Clearly, the level or standard to which the historical study is aimed will to a large extent determine both the suitability of the project and the breadth and depth of the investigations.

The Yorkshire spa town of Harrogate is taken here as an example, and this was identified for study in the knowledge that 'spas' or 'watering places' are historically reputed for their social activities of which dancing was an integral and important feature. The social life of the South of England spas such as Bath and Cheltenham is fairly well documented but, although the North of England spas are frequently referred to, little seems to be known of their dancing activities. The aim of the investigation, therefore, was to discover whether this Yorkshire Spa would prove to be characteristically similar to other better-known spas in terms of social dance trends. It is possible that the processes outlined here could be applied to historical studies in other towns or districts.

The study was set against the background of the nineteenth century as it was evident that Harrogate grew and developed as a fashionable spa during this period. The architecture itself is indicative of Harrogate's emergence from two small villages in the Georgian period to a prosperous Victorian town by the end of the century. The vast common lying between the two villages, which Smollett (1771) referred to 'as a wild common, bare and bleak, without a tree or shrub or the least signs of cultivation', was divided by the railway line built in 1862. The railway station provided a focus for the growth of the central area of Harrogate during the Victorian period and the street developments which followed are in the Victorian style. The picture is further enhanced by a statue of Queen Victoria erected at the time of her Golden Jubilee in 1887, which even now firmly dominates the town centre.

6.1 *Locating source material*

Locating source material can be unpredictable. The most relevant historical documentation is not always to be found in the most obvious places, as indicated by some of the examples given in this section. Nevertheless, the element of chance can be an important and exciting aspect of the search. The insights gained, for example, by a chance discussion with a local history enthusiast or the discovery of a hitherto unmentioned publication on a musty library shelf often outweigh the disappointment of a predetermined lead which failed to provide any evidence. This, of course, does not diminish the importance of a pre-structured line of enquiry based on identifiable regional sources. Indeed, it simply serves to endorse the *value* of such sources in providing evidence for the existence of dance and the context within which previously uncollated material may be placed.

During the preliminary enquiries made in Harrogate for this particular study, references to source material not apparently available in Harrogate itself led to a wider search for material through other possible regional sources outside the immediate locality. To some extent this characterises the *nature* of regional sources in that for various practical reasons, e.g. the movement of material from one place to another, the search may extend beyond the physical boundaries initially selected. Therefore the increasing expansion of urban boundaries into rural districts can sometimes pose difficulties for the researcher in locating source material.

6.2 *Harrogate sources*

Valuable sources of historical documentation were located in the reference section of the *Harrogate Library* which contained a considerable amount of *primary* and *secondary source material*. Initial setbacks were, however, encountered in the case of some of the other Harrogate sources.

The present Assembly Rooms were not built until 1897 and therefore are clearly unrepresentative of the social life of the earlier part of the century, but there was evidence of an earlier Assembly Room known as the Royal Promenade and Cheltenham Pump Room. This building, built by a private owner in 1835, had been situated on another site and was demolished in 1939 to make way for a more up-to-date concert hall now known as the Royal Hall. Unfortunately, all that visually remains of the building are some colonnades, situated in the Harlow Car Gardens, and some prints and photographs taken at various stages during its brief history. Many written descriptions of the building were located, however, and these provide the main source of evidence for the existence of this grand 'salon'. It is also known that the building changed ownership during its brief history moving from private to municipal ownership by the end of the nineteenth century. It is possible that architectural records and conveyancing documents may still be in existence and that these could possibly provide a further source for investigation.

The local *Newspaper Offices* also proved disappointing since, although copies of the nineteenth century newspapers were held there, they were not easily accessible to the public. The situation necessitated a newspaper employee carrying the leather-bound folders of newspapers from a storage place in another building. This was impracticable in view of the large amount of bulky material involved and particularly as it was known by this stage that back-dated copies, though not in complete sets, were held at the local library and were more easily accessible.

6.3 *Other regional sources relating to Harrogate*

Because of the lack of storage space at Harrogate Library some documentation on Harrogate's past had been transferred to the *Archives Department of the North Yorkshire County Records Office* at Northallerton. Storage space is a universal problem and it must be assumed that it is not uncommon for local source material to be moved to a regional central office. This can, of course, lead to difficulties in gaining access to source material and as a result could limit the extent to which the research is carried out. Undoubtedly, it is necessary to contact the archivist requesting permission to visit, which also implies a prior knowledge of the existence of certain documentation if it is to be identified from amongst the vast amount of regional material.

In this case, a visit to the County Records Office proved negative as the particular diary requested, known as the Greeves Diary written by a Harrogate surveyor around 1842 and thought to contain a reference to dance was unavailable, possibly missing. Thus even when primary source materials are known it does not follow that they can be located or are readily available.

Further difficulties were experienced in tracing Dr Augustus Granville's three-volume document, *Spas of England* (1841), which was cited by a number of authors as being a primary text on nineteenth century spas. A damaged, but original part-volume was eventually found in the Brotherton Library, Leeds, but sadly not the part which was relevant to North of England spas. In the circumstances, there was no alternative but to use a later edition of the work located in the same library. It is possible that conflicting evidence may occur in instances where more than one edition of an author's work has been published over a period of time. A second or subsequent edition may be altered in certain details and, although this is not the place for any detailed discussion of the problem, in some situations an examination of the first and later editions of a publication can in itself be a valid tool for historical research.

Despite initial setbacks in the Harrogate researches, relevant documentation, in addition to that located in the Harrogate Reference Library, was also discovered in the Leeds City Reference Library. City Reference Libraries frequently contain material on aspects of regional topographical interest and are always worth a visit. It is also not unusual for *private book collections* to be bequeathed to local libraries within the locality in which the collector lived. It may not be beyond the realms of possibility that valuable collections on specific subjects, such as local history, or even dance, may be available through a local reference library or other such library. In this case a specially arranged visit to the Leeds Private Library, which has a membership by subscription, revealed an interesting though not rare source of eighteenth and nineteenth century dance books.

6.4 *Regional source material on Harrogate*

Faced with a wide variety of possible regional sources, two major factors were important in *evaluating* the source material relevant to this historical study:

1. to identify material which was characteristic of the social dance of the period;
2. to identify material which characterised the particular nature of the Harrogate Spa.

The examples of regional sources given here can be seen to correspond with the *written, visual* and *aural* categories already outlined in Chapter 2 although additional sources are also included.

For clarification purposes the sources used in this particular historical study have been divided into those which proved most valuable in providing evidence for the existence of dance and those which were informative on the social and historical background of the Harrogate Spa. Although the distinction between the dance and the context in which it arose, in this case Harrogate Spa, is useful it cannot always be maintained in discussion. In some instances the reference to the Harrogate Spa social life took on an unusual significance which clearly had wider consequences for the study of dance within this historical context.

Reference material relating to general nineteenth-century history was helpful in gaining some understanding of the historical background to the period, although no detailed study was considered necessary. It was nevertheless useful to recognise, for example, that the increased growth and expansion which took place in the Victorian period in Harrogate was just one aspect of the increasing prosperity and greater social mobility which was reflected within the wider macrocosm of society as a whole.

Spa histories (see References, p. 112) also proved useful in providing comparative accounts of the varied geographical positions and social amenities afforded by spa resorts, while source material relating specifically to the social dance trends of this period (see References) provided a basis on which to assess evidence for dance at Harrogate.

The model which follows lists examples of primary and secondary source material which was used in this particular historical study. It will be seen that certain sources are placed in both the dance history and spa history categories. Written sources, such as the general spa histories, provided historical information on both the development of the Harrogate Spa and on social dance.

Examples of regional source material used as evidence for the existence of social dance in the Yorkshire spa town of Harrogate

Secondary Source Material	Primary Source Material
Social Dance	**Social Dance**
written sources: local histories, spa histories	written sources: diaries, fictional accounts, medical treatises, newspaper articles, advertisements, spa histories, street directories
visual sources: prints	
oral sources: none	
	visual sources: ball cards, dance invitation cards, prints
Harrogate Spa	**Harrogate Spa**
written sources: local histories, spa histories	written sources: almanacs, local histories, newspapers, spa histories, street directories, topographies, visitors' guides
visual sources: buildings, maps, photographs, prints	
oral sources: people with local knowledge including descendants from known Harrogate residents, local history enthusiasts	visual sources: maps, prints

6.5 *Secondary source material*

The secondary source examples discussed here were valuable for several reasons. Some of the *written sources*, such as local histories, had drawn their material from existing *primary sources* and, therefore, provided a variety of references from which to make further research. Jennings' edited history (1970) is a good example here as it consists of material compiled by a number of local history enthusiasts, and as their sources are well documented it can be assumed that their evidence is reliable.

It was possible from *visual sources*, such as buildings, prints and photographs, to piece together a picture of the development of the town from the early Georgian period to the end of the century. From this visual material it was also possible to identify the architectural features of the 1835 Royal Promenade and Cheltenham Pump Room and, combined with the written descriptions of these particular Assembly Rooms, to gain some understanding of the style of this unique social centre.

People, too, provided interesting *oral accounts* of Harrogate's past. A local Harrogate doctor, for instance, gave a lively and enthusiastic description of the 'practices' of the Victorian spa doctors. The custom was for the visitor to select a doctor from among the many portraits which hung in the various chemist shops. The visitor would then consult him at his rooms as to the most appropriate 'cure'. Disappointingly, nobody was discovered whose enthusiastic memories extended to a well known dancing master or a celebratory ball! The fact that such people were not located, however, does not preclude the possibility of their existence.

6.6 *Primary source material*

The primary sources discussed here are taken in a sequence designed to give the most coherent account and are not placed in any chronological order of historical events. Attention is given to specific items of primary source material since these made a particularly valuable contribution to the study.

Newspapers proved to be a significant source of material in tracing the growth and development of the Harrogate Spa but, more importantly, provided valuable evidence for the existence of dance in the form of articles, advertisements and published prints.

The founding and development of the Harrogate newspapers themselves is historically interesting. The *Pallisers List of Weekly Visitors* was first established in 1835 and was printed in May prior to the start of the Season, which at that time was in July and August. It is evident from this source that social activities mainly centred around those two months in the year when visitors congregated at the Spa. By 1840 the paper became known as the *Harrogate Advertiser* and gradually began to report on events of both local and national interest. In 1847 a rival paper was set up known as the *Harrogate Herald*, but the *Advertiser* was the more informative on social events, especially those which took place at the Royal Promenade and Cheltenham Pump Room.

The discovery of the following note, published in the *Pallisers List of Weekly Visitors* 25 July 1835, provided the first indication of the existence of these particular Assembly Rooms:

> The style of this superb edifice, whether we regard its external or its internal structure is preeminently superior to any similar erection in the neighbourhood having been built at the expense of several thousand pounds and being capable of accommodating upwards of 500 persons. The proprietor contemplates that every arrangement for its completion will be effected previous to 21st August next, his most gracious Majesty's birthday, on which occasion it is his intention to gratify the expectation of the public by giving a splendid public ball.

A few days prior to the official opening on August 17th, another advertisement appeared:

> In addition to the Band of the Scots Greys, the proprietor has engaged an eminent Quadrille Band. The surrounding gardens and pleasure ground will be elegantly illuminated with variegated lamps, after the style of Vauxhall Gardens, London.

A contemporary account of the events which actually took place at the grand opening ball was not discovered, but certain conclusions were nevertheless drawn from the advertisements. For instance, although the building had been styled in the mode of its earlier eighteenth century counterparts, the reference to Vauxhall Gardens, London, also suggests that perhaps certain features had been included to make it more fashionable and up-to-date in terms of nineteenth century social trends. The fact that a quadrille band had been engaged for the occasion was also a good indication that the dances were compatible with other general dance trends at that time, quadrilles, for example, being at the peak of fashion (see Richardson 1960).

Evidence from newspaper articles and from other sources, discussed elsewhere in this chapter, shows that dancing also took place at various venues in addition to the Royal Promenade and Cheltenham Pump Room. It would seem that prior to the opening of the 1835 Assembly Rooms, social dancing had been a feature of the hotels and inns, an inheritance from the eighteenth century. This social pattern continued throughout the nineteenth century when the custom was to rotate the dances between several hotels, an arrangement which no doubt suited the hoteliers for obvious commercial reasons.

During the mid part of the century fresh evidence for the existence of social dance at Harrogate began to appear in the form of newspaper advertisements.

> Fashionable Readers – Our readers – we are sure, will be pleased to know that Mr Nicholas Henderson of London, whose name, from the fact of Mr Henderson having introduced Cellarius and several other beautiful waltzes into the fashionable circles of the metropolis has recently become so popular, is now in Harrogate, and purposes remaining during the season. To those who desire to become acquainted with the latest exportations in this delightful art which not to know is to be excluded from the assemblies of the select – will, we doubt not, avail themselves of the abilities of a gentleman whose style is much appreciated by the elite in London and elsewhere.
>
> (*Harrogate Advertiser*, 15 July 1848)

Approximately two weeks later Mr Henderson duly presented himself as follows:

> Mr Nicholas Henderson (from 19 Newman Street London) begs respectfully to inform the nobility and gentry of Harrogate, that he has just arrived for a limited period, and purposes teaching all the new and fashionable dances, as danced by his pupils at Almacks, and the nobility balls in London.
>
> The Polka, Schottische, Valse à deux Temps, Redowa, etc., in three lessons. One guinea. Schools and families attended. 10 Waterloo Terrace, Low Harrogate.
>
> (*Harrogate Advertiser*, 29 July 1848)

These particular advertisements provided certain missing clues which had not previously materialised through other sources referred to later. For example, no significant reference had been found prior to this date of the existence of a resident dancing master in Harrogate. The advertisements would appear to substantiate the opinion that perhaps no resident dancing master of any note did in fact exist in Harrogate at this time as it would seem improbable that Mr Henderson would have been in a position to offer his services had any substantial local competition been available.

Other explanations for the apparent paucity of Harrogate dancing masters are possible. It is known, for example, that three dancing academies existed in the nearby city of Leeds and it is possible that local Harrogate residents were serviced by these, although this is as yet only a speculation.

The fact that a London dancing master, apparently of good repute, considered it worthwhile to set up business in a Northern spa town during a Harrogate season is in itself indicative of the extent to which social dancing had taken serious purchase. His fee of one guinea for three lessons is also worth noting, as although no direct evidence of charges for dance lessons in London in the same period was discovered, valuable regional evidence in the form of the Fawcett papers (1970) indicates that the price for lessons in Norwich in 1819 was 'two lessons a week for one guinea per quarter'. In the light of this information, even taking account of possible rises in fees, it would appear that Mr Henderson's prices were quite high. Finally, if it can be assumed that Mr Henderson did actually teach the dances he mentions in his advertisement, then it is possible to conclude that social dancing at Harrogate was compatible with the popular social dance trends of the period put forward by the leading dance historians (see References).

6.7 *Harrogate histories*

Useful comparative information on Harrogate's development as a spa was available in a number of histories of Harrogate written in the nineteenth century (see References).

Historical research is frequently dependent upon descriptions of historical events which have to be interpreted, and in the light of this, knowledge of the authors themselves, where this is available, can sometimes be an important factor in assessing the *reliability* of their source material.

William Grainge, for example, was a known Harrogate resident in the nineteenth century and wrote extensively on local history and it can therefore be assumed that his local knowledge was fairly sound. Similarly, Dr Augustus Granville was considered to be somewhat of an influential authority on spas in the nineteenth century having travelled extensively visiting the English and German resorts. His observations were mainly directed towards the medicinal aspects of the spas, but he does, nevertheless, *unwittingly*, make many significant comments on the social life-styles of the spas. On a visit to Harrogate in 1839 in preparation for his book *Spas of England*, Granville provides an interesting account of an 'impromptu ball' at the Royal Promenade and Cheltenham Pump Room:

> The Doric Temple showed off to great advantage by night, like many of the ladies who figured it; and with a superior company, such as we meet here at a more advanced period of the season, a ball, in it must be a mighty fine thing for killing time at Harrogate. The place was not crowded; but a good sprinkling of people of almost every sort was scattered over the floor, or occupied the different ottomans in the recesses. Some were dressed as for an evening party, for there had been sufficient notice given in the afternoon of this impromptu. Others had not thought it worth while to go home to dress, and the ladies appeared 'sans façon', in morning bonnets, with their partners en frac. Amidst these heterogeneous groups, the six or eight stewards, with their white rosettes and smart coats, appeared like so many turkey-trots strutting among the motley inhabitants of la basse cour.
>
> (vol. 1, pp. 47–8)

The impression is gained from Granville's description of the ball that it was a fairly informal affair, held during the early part of the season and attended by an 'assortment' of people. It is also possible that the manager of the Royal Promenade and Cheltenham Pump Room may have seized the opportunity of Granville's visit to profit by an 'impromptu ball' at a time of the year when the season had barely started. The manager would also, no doubt, have been aware that Granville's future publication might present some favourable remarks on the Assembly Rooms which, due to it being somewhat of a late-comer in comparison with other spa Assembly Rooms, had not to that date been referred to in any of the general literature on spa resorts. Certainly, Granville's comments on these magnificent rooms were indeed praiseworthy and he also observed that the only significant social attraction at Harrogate was dancing, which he clearly viewed with approval.

Wheater (1890) provides a further example of an author who at the same time as communicating historical information also *unwittingly* comments on aspects of spa social life. Although Wheater was writing in the nineteenth century, his observations reflect the eighteenth century period. It appeared that during the eighteenth century the Harrogate Spa had developed a respectable reputation in comparison with other more fashionable resorts. Wheater attributes Harrogate's soberness to the fact that: 'Harrogate never had a Beau Nash or a Captain Webster to corrupt it'. This arrangement is clearly approved by Wheater, as he goes on to explain:

> At no time are we able to trace in Harrogate the existence of a Long Room or Assembly Room separate and apart from an hotel. The value to decorum of such an arrangement is obvious to all who have studied the lives of the beaux. Scarborough and Bath placed their society in the hands of Masters of the Ceremonies, but no such creatures were ever known in Harrogate. Scarborough had her notorious beau, Tristram Fishe. The vagaries of this Long Room eclipsed even those of Bath when card swindling was added to their other foibles.

The Masters of Ceremonies to which Wheater refers were notable luminaries of spa assemblies in the eighteenth century, one of their functions being to uphold the etiquette of the ballroom. It is evident that the role of Master of Ceremony continued well into the nineteenth century. The possible ramifications for social dance at Harrogate in the absence of such a professional person are self-evident and the question arises as to how the social dance functions were officiated. Feltham (1824) provides a possible explanation.

> The Master of Ceremonies is elected by the company, of whom he is always one; and he retains his rank during his stay, when another gentleman is chosen in his rooms. To this office, good manners and a suavity of disposition are the only pass-ports; no intrigues, no solicitations are used to procure this appointment:– it is offered as a voluntary compliment to him who appears to deserve it best, and it is discharged without fee or emolument: the only reward, and it is enough to every generous heart, is the reflection that this distinction has been merited to be allowed.

This implies that there must have been members of the 'company', i.e. spa visitors, who were sufficiently well versed in the etiquette of the ballroom to take on such office. The impermanence of the office of Master of Ceremony created a transient situation which would not, presumably, have allowed for the scandals of the beaux of Bath and other notorious watering places to gain foothold in Harrogate. Even the advent of the Royal Promenade and Cheltenham Pump Room did not lead to the appointment of a Master of Ceremonies, although it can be assumed that the manager of these Assembly Rooms would have adopted the role when the situation demanded.

In the light of Wheater's information and other source material, it is open to argument whether Harrogate's early speculators avoided such social problems by precluding the appointment of a professional Master of Ceremonies. The fact that Harrogate developed as a latter-day spa would have, no doubt, enabled lessons to be learned from the mistakes of other spas. A likely explanation for the absence of a professional Master of Ceremonies, however, would seem to be that by the nineteenth century the social pattern which had grown out of existing resources, such as the inns, hotels and local musicians, was by now too firmly established for any radical change to take place.

Diaries, written by some of Harrogate's past leading visitors and residents provided a number of interesting first-hand accounts on aspects of spa life. Some of this material was, however, irrelevant to this particular historical study and the whereabouts of the Greeves Diary (see p. 98), which may have proved more informative, remained a mystery.

The most significant diary item which relates to the Regency period was discovered in the Smith Manuscript (1816), so called because only part of the original diary has survived. Smith provides a detailed contemporary account of his impressions of the ball-nights held at the Crown hotel during his Harrogate stay. Although he does not specifically mention the dancing he does draw attention to some interesting features.

> On Ball nights the drawing room is lit up with flame lit candles – and the charge is 2/6 per head, which includes negus. There is one ball in each principal house every week and generally a private dance on some intervening evening day, when you only pay a shilling. Invitations

are usually sent by card from one to the other, requesting the favour of each others company on the ball nights.

The ball nights in August were Monday at the Dragon, Wednesday at the Crown, Thursday at the Queens Head, Friday at the Granby – The private dances at the Crown were on Saturdays. The master of the inn charges the waiter for the candles, from 2–4d. indeed the charge is as he pleases, for he obliges the waiter to tell the number of half crowns he gets, (for the purchase money is the waiters) and then he puts on accordingly for the candles, which generally last 3 nights, on one of which is a private dance for which the master charges one shilling per head. The waiter also pays about 7d. each to five musicians; one of whom is an excellent harpist.

Much of Smith's attention is centred on the cost of dances, a point which, though not pursued here, could prove to be of some relevance as a yardstick for assessing the relative importance of dance as a social activity compared with other activities and other spas.

Smith's reference to the custom of sending *invitation cards* from one 'principal' house to another highlights a further possible area for investigation. The fact that Smith differentiates between the 'ball nights' held at the 'principal hotels' and the 'private dances' which were apparently held for the benefit of the residents of the individual hotels is interesting. It is reasonable to assume that the presentation of these invitations was designed to exclude other lodging houses of a lesser standing and in this way keep the company elite and respectable. It is open to speculation as to whether the cost of 2/6 (12½p) per head, in addition to candle charges, may also have been an added prohibitive factor.

It is possible that this source material could be of further use in another study with a different objective, such as to establish the relationship between social class and the type of dance performed. Its value to this particular study is in the factual contribution it makes to the whole in that pertinent facts emerged which enabled certain conclusions to be drawn.

An interesting and unusual *fictional account* of a social season at Harrogate during the Regency period exists in the form of Barbara Hofland's book, *A Season at Harrogate* (1812).

The book, which is written in verse, takes the form of a series of letters written by the character Benjamin Blunderhead to his mother, concerning his activities during a stay at the Harrogate Spa. Despite the fact that the story is fictitious it is nevertheless worth noting, in view of the knowledge which is available about the author. The *Harrogate Advertiser* (16 April 1960) indicates that Hofland came to Harrogate in 1809 as Mrs Hoole, a widow in her early thirties. Needing to support herself, she began teaching and took over a girls' boarding school at Grove House, where, for financial reasons, she also accommodated paying guests. She later married T. C. Hofland, the artist. The newspaper article already cited intimates that Hofland wanted her book to be profitable and therefore 'made it more palatable to the general reader by presenting it in the guise of a romantic love story'. Unlike some authors, such as Jane Austen who embellished her stories by setting them against the background of a spa, Hofland utilises the story as a convenient framework into which she weaves her realistic images of life at the spa. It is probable that the context of Hofland's account is authentic, since it is based on her observations of the residents and visitors to Harrogate.

Hofland adds colour to her bright young hero Blunderhead by making him a keen dancer. His obvious love of dancing thereby enables her to 'wax lyrical' in her descriptions of some of the other characters present at the dances. The literary device employed here by Hofland affords her the opportunity of narrating what was obviously an important social pastime during this period, namely dancing.

Obviously this source material does not in isolation constitute evidence for the existence of dance at Harrogate because its fictional basis must be taken into account. Nevertheless, in the light of what has already been outlined it does represent an added dimension which, combined with evidence from other sources, provides fresh insights into the level of socialisation which might have taken place during this period.

Medical treatises were ignored in the initial stages of the study as they were thought to be purely of scientific interest. However, later in the researches, and partly as a result of the conversation with the Harrogate doctor already mentioned, this unexpected source of evidence for social dance was discovered. It is important, therefore, in the preliminary examination of primary sources to scan *all* the material available and not to prejudge the worth of any source.

An examination of these documents revealed some fascinating hints on the practice and benefits derived from 'spawing', i.e. participating in spa-life, of which physical exercise was referred to as an important aspect. The following extract from a nineteenth century medical treatise gives a clear indication of the attitudes which this Victorian doctor held towards dancing as a means to good health in body and mind:

> Than dancing, there is no species of exercise which can be taken within doors more cheering to the mind, and renovating to the body; and though usually considered a fatiguing recreation, it seldom produces any bad consequences. The music alone has remarkable power over many individuals in soothing the mind and equalizing the passions; and a placid state of mind becomes in turn a powerful auxilary in the treatment and cure of no small number of the most inveterate diseases. The weak and delicate ought not to exert themselves like the strong and vigorous and in no instance should the body when overheated be suddenly exposed to the cold air. The warm bath though from the usages of society rarely compatible with dancing hours, is a real luxury after this exercise, and will frequently induce sound and tranquil sleep.
>
> (Hunter, 1846, p. 174)

This particular evidence is significant in that it reflects some of the popular justifications for social dancing during the nineteenth century, namely, that dancing should not only be regarded as a social pastime, but also valued for its beneficial effect on the physical well-being.

The view put forward by established dance historians already cited suggests that in comparison with the eighteenth century, dancing became less popular towards the end of the nineteenth century in that it was no longer considered as a necessary social accomplishment. It is reasonable therefore to assume that these same attitudes would have had an effect on the social activities of the spas and that those seeking a more serious approach to their social life would find in Hunter's recommendations on dancing an 'ideal recipe' for social indulgence.

It is known that the Evangelical Movement had a fairly strong influence in the mid part of the nineteenth century and that a group was actively at work in Harrogate in 1841. It is possible that a more detailed study of the effects of various socialising agents over a period of time and the shifts of attitudes which occurred as a result, may be a worthwhile area for a future historical study.

It is also evident that medical treatises provide a unique form of source material on dance, and as such, could provide a further area for investigation of dance history, which could have a national rather than a regional focus.

Street Directories, like parish registers, can provide useful sources of information. Before the advent of telephone and *Yellow Pages* directories, street directories frequently acted as professional registers listing names, addresses and professional occupations of private individuals as well as commercial business enterprises.

It is likely that 'dancing masters' would also have used this outlet as a means of advertising their professional role. However, an examination of the nineteenth century directories revealed, in this case, only one name which was of any relevance:

Coverdale, J.   7 Gladstone Street, Commercial teacher
and professor of dancing.
(Harrogate Directory 1877, p. 19)

No further reference to this particular person was discovered and the same street directories did not reveal any other named dancing masters. This information was nevertheless of value in that, combined with evidence from other sources, it served to underline the point made previously that no well-known Harrogate dancing master existed during this period.

Conclusions

The regional evidence used in the Harrogate study showed that the social dance activities were, to some extent, idiosyncratic when compared with other documented spa assemblies of the same period.

Harrogate was .characteristically different from other prototype spa towns such as Bath and Cheltenham in that it did not have Assembly Rooms until 1835. The late-coming of the Assembly Rooms also undoubtedly contributed to the absence of any known professional Master of Ceremonies, a feature which further distinguished Harrogate from its counterparts.

It would seem that while Harrogate emulated the social dance trends of the period, following in the wake of the popular dances of London and elsewhere, it did so within the context of its own resources.

Social dancing at Harrogate established itself in the inns and later continued to develop in the new hotels as these emerged, a pattern which carried on throughout the nineteenth century. The Royal Promenade and Cheltenham Pump Room built in 1835 provided an additional venue for dancing on a larger and grander scale, which no doubt added a further dimension to the dance activities and balls which took place at Harrogate.

The Harrogate study underlines the regional individuality evident in the patterns for social dancing at this particular spa in the nineteenth century. Such a conclusion could only be stated on the basis of a study in which a thorough search and analysis of regional sources had been undertaken and the regional evidence then studied within the national context. Further investigations of other localities using regional source material would, similarly, highlight the distinctiveness and significance of geographical location in the historical study of dance.

References

Addison, W. 1951 *English spas.* London: B.T. Batsford

Fawcett, T. 1970 'Provincial Dancing Masters', *Norfolk archaeology*, vol. XXXV, part 1

Feltham, J. 1824 *A guide to all watering and sea-bathing places.* London: Richard Phillips

*Fletcher, J. S. 1920 *Harrogate and Knaresborough.* New York: Macmillan

øFranks, A. H. 1963 *Social dance: a short history.* London: Routledge & Kegan Paul

Grainge, W. 1871 *The history and topography of Harrogate and the Forest of Knaresborough.* London: Smith

Grainge, W. 1875 *A guide to Harrogate and visitors' handbook.* Pately Bridge: Thomas Thorpe

Granville, A. B. 1841 *Spas of England and principal sea-bathing places* (2 vols.). London: Henry Colburn

*Grove, L. (ed.) 1895 *Dancing.* London: Longmans & Green

Harrogate Advertiser 1839–79 Harrogate: Robert Ackrill

Harrogate Directory 1877 Harrogate: J. L. Armstrong

øHaythornthwaite, W. 1954 *Harrogate story: From Georgian village to Victorian town.* Yorkshire: The Dalesman Publishing Company

Hofland, B. 1812 *A season at Harrogate in a series of poetical epistles.* Harrogate: R. Wilson

Hunter, A. 1846 *A treatise on the waters of Harrogate and its vicinity* London: Longman

Jennings, B. (ed.) 1970 *A history of Harrogate and Knaresborough.* Huddersfield: Advertiser Press

*Lennard, R. (ed.) 1931 *An Englishman at rest and play: Some phases of English leisure, 1558–1714.* Oxford: Clarendon Press

*Luke, T. D. 1919 *Spas and health resorts of the British Isles.* London: A. & C. Black

Pallisers List of Weekly Visitors 1835 Harrogate: Pickersgill Palliser

øPatmore, J. A. 1963 *An atlas of Harrogate.* Oxford: Alden Press

øPiggot, G. W. R. 1865 *The Harrogate Spas.* Harrogate: Thomas Hollins

*Pimlott, J. A. R. 1947 *An Englishman's holiday.* London: Faber

Richardson, P. J. S. 1960 *The social dances of the nineteenth century.* London, Herbert Jenkins

øRust, F. 1969 *Dance in society.* London: Routledge & Kegan Paul

*Scott, E. 1892 *Dancing as an art and pastime.* London: Bell

Smith, D. W. & daughters 1816 Notes of visits to Harrogate in 1816. Harrogate Reference Library

Smollett, T. 1771 *The expedition of Humphrey Clinker.* Milford: Oxford University Press

Wheater, W. (1890) *A guide to and history of Harrogate: Its story grave and gay.* Leeds: Goodall and Suddick

* not directly referred to in text, but useful reading

ø referred to in text but authors not named, e.g. nineteenth century historians, dance historians

PART III

Approaches to historical study based on different forms of dance

In Part III the examples of historical study are derived from the diverse nature of each of three forms of dance, classical ballet in the European tradition; modern dance, in its early European stage; and traditional dance, in its English ceremonial and social forms.

This is, in a sense, to start from the other end of a process from looking at sources and to ask questions about one form of dance, perhaps about its development through time, to isolate significant changes and to ask what the reasons were for its evolution. Each of these three forms of dance provides a vast range of possible study areas. Depending upon the choice of focus, a methodology can be developed. Each chapter in this part describes such possibilities.

CHAPTER 7

Classical ballet, the European tradition

by Patricia A. Mitchinson

7.1 Ballet companies
7.2 Repertory
7.3 Choreography based on Shakespearian themes with particular reference to *Romeo and Juliet*
7.4 MacMillan's *Romeo and Juliet*
7.5 Examples of twentieth century ballets based on Shakespeare's *Romeo and Juliet*

The historical significance of classical ballet as a dance form is well documented by both past and present historians and its contribution to the development of dance as a theatre art in the Western world is unquestioned.

A study of any period in the history of classical ballet will show that while its initial development was subject to the principles of 'classicism', its subsequent evolution has been dependent upon the innovations brought about by its protagonists and by external influences within art and society. As an example the 'spirit of Romanticism', reflected in art as a whole in the early nineteenth century, was a motivating force in the development of classical ballet. During this period, known as the *Romantic*, the classical ballet technique as described in Carlo Blasis' treatise (1820) was further extended to incorporate dancing *en pointe*. The significance of this development in ballet technique, found in *La Sylphide* a ballet created for Marie Taglioni in 1832, was to revolutionise the aesthetic of classical ballet. Thus, in a period which was concerned with the expression of the 'unearthly' and 'spiritual' elements as part of its aesthetic, the effect of dancing *en pointe* considerably enhanced the elevated haunting lightness of 'sylph-like creatures' such as the Wilis in Act 2 of *Giselle*.

116

The length of the classical ballet tradition provides a richness and diversity of material for historical consideration. The development of the classical ballet technique is one potential area of study. Evidence of a multiplicity of forms exists in the variety of approaches to the study and teaching of classical ballet at the present time*. Attention is given here, however, to other characteristic features of this dance form as it exists within the context of the twentieth century. Sections 7.1 and 7.2 deal with the ballet companies in the European tradition and their repertories and sections 7.3, 7.4 and 7.5 give consideration to a narrative source which has been of special interest to choreographers in this century, namely the use of Shakespearian themes. Special reference is made to *Romeo and Juliet*, particularly MacMillan's version.

7.1 *Ballet companies*

There are a number of different types of ballet companies in various parts of Europe each with their own distinctive features. Clarke and Crisp (1981) provide a helpful overview of the major ballet companies in this country and other parts of Europe and point to historical events and people who have been instrumental in their development†.

The existence of ballet companies in any country is dependent to a large extent on government funding policies and attitudes towards centralisation and regionalisation of the arts. A study of the emergence, development and decline of ballet companies in Britain since the end of World War II, for example, would undoubtedly reveal a number of changing patterns. The current scene in Britain shows a wide spectrum of classical companies. Examples of major companies in London include the *Royal Ballet*, resident at the Royal Opera House, the *Sadler's Wells Royal Ballet* touring company and the *London Festival Ballet* which maintains its tradition as a large-scale touring company. The *Ballet Rambert* is a unique example of a major dance company which, while founded on a tradition of

---

* The Gulbenkian Report (1980) points to the widely differing schools and organisations in existence in this country which cover a broad spectrum of training in classical ballet.

†For further useful information on the background of European Ballet, see Brinson 1966, Brinson & Crisp 1980, Guest 1960.

classical ballet, currently has a repertory almost entirely devoted to works in the contemporary dance idiom. Outside London there are companies in Scotland and Wales of which the *Scottish Ballet*, formerly Western Theatre Ballet, has now achieved large-scale recognition. Compared with the field of contemporary dance, there are relatively few small ballet companies: *Northern Ballet Theatre* is an example of a well-established regionally based company and currently there are a number of smaller companies such as the *Genée Ballet, London City Ballet* and the *Alexander Roy London Ballet Theatre*.

The discussion here centres on the characteristics of traditional-style ballet companies which typify the European tradition as it exists today. Examples of major European ballet companies, such as our own *Royal Ballet*, the *Royal Danish Ballet*, the *Paris Opera Ballet* are, for historical reasons, regarded as national ballet companies: a prestigious status which distinguishes them as monumental examples of the classical ballet tradition. Characteristically, this type of company is attached to a state theatre or opera house which provides a permanent place to rehearse and perform. Permanence, therefore, is a particular feature of this category of company which is founded on an established centre of dance excellence. The company school to which young dancers are recruited provides a supporting structure which enables the historic tradition and a consistency of artistic style to be maintained from school to company. A company of this nature consists of a network of people: dancers, choreographers, teachers, musicians, administrators and technicians. There is a definable hierarchy of dancers which functions on the traditional 'star system' and incorporates principals, soloists, coryphées and corps de ballet.

The migration of dancers and choreographers is historically significant in the development of dance as a theatre art. In previous centuries, as at the present time, it was not uncommon for dancers to achieve recognition in countries outside their country of origin. In 1734 the French dancer Marie Sallé was popular with London audiences and the achievements of the French choreographer and theorist Jean-Georges Noverre (1727–1810) are evident in a number of dance centres of the world, notably Paris, London, Stuttgart and Vienna. In the nineteenth century, when the focus for dance excellence was centred in St Petersburg, Russia, Italian dancers who worked there were noted for the brilliance of their technique.

The channels through which the process of cultural interaction

118

takes place today is little changed. It is not uncommon for dancers and choreographers to spend time working abroad with other companies. For example, Kenneth MacMillan, the English choreographer, created the ballet *Song of the Earth* to Mahler's music for the Stuttgart Ballet in 1965. Similarly, Royal Ballet's Lynn Seymour was Prima Ballerina to the German Opera Ballet in Berlin between 1966–69. Gow (1979) gives an account of a short-term exchange which took place between Royal Ballet teacher Terry Westmoreland and Paris Opera Ballet's Gilbert Mayer in 1979. In the article he highlights one of the benefits of this aspect of cultural exchange in that dancers have the opportunity of broadening the scope of their dance skills by adapting to different stylistic approaches in the classical ballet technique. More recently, in 1982, Mona Vangsaae from the Royal Danish Ballet was a guest teacher at the Royal Ballet School. Mona Vangsaae also staged a Royal Ballet Covent Garden production of *Konservatoriet*, in which pupils of the Royal Ballet Junior School took part (Clarke, 1983). This ballet was originally created by the Danish choreographer August Bournonville in 1849 and therefore reflects the 'Bournonville style' which has been influential in the development of the Royal Danish Ballet. Thus in the case of *Konservatoriet* Mona Vangsaae provided a significant link between the Royal Ballet Company and the Bournonville tradition as it exists today in the Royal Danish Ballet.

The Artistic Director is the person who is responsible for maintaining the traditions of the ballet company as well as initiating fresh directions. The planning and organisation of a company repertory is complex and the artistic policy may be influenced by a number of factors, such as financial success, as well as artistic criteria. Ballet companies attached to major European Opera Houses may not be in a position to take artistic risks which could result in poor financial return. Thus, in contrast to smaller companies whose repertory might include ballets of a more experimental nature, the repertory of a large scale company might be characterised as the presentation of works by well-established choreographers. Traditional classic ballets such as *Swan Lake* (1877) invariably form the backbone of the repertories of these major classical ballet companies.

7.2 *Repertory*

A ballet company is judged by the quality of its repertory and to a large degree is dependent upon achieving a balance between upholding and furthering the classical tradition. The repertory is the product by which a company's artistic standards are assessed; it gives an indication of the length of that company's tradition and its links with the past. It would therefore be possible to study the work of different artists such as choreographers, dancers, designers, musical composers, either individually or collectively in any one historical period and from this to identify the development of a company's tradition. There are also examples of European choreographers whose associations with particular companies could be investigated: Cranko's link with the Stuttgart Ballet, the Bournonville influence, as reflected in the repertory of the Royal Danish Ballet, and the establishment of the so-called English style through Ashton's involvement with the Royal Ballet in this country.

Ballets constitute the repertory, and the elements which make up the ballet as a whole are the choreography, librettos, musical scores and designs. Each of these constituents can be studied in an historical context by referring to evidence such as programme notes from actual performances and critical reviews. Examples of the types of ballets which might be characteristically associated with major classical ballet companies are discussed in the next section and are grouped as follows:

7.2.1 The common heritage – a shared tradition of ballets such as *Giselle* (1841) and *Swan Lake* (1895)

7.2.2 A unique contribution – ballets which are distinctively associated with individial company repertories thus contributing to the unique character of a company's repertory.

7.2.3 Contemporary ballets – new works commissioned by a ballet company

7.2.4 Ballet revivals

7.2.1. *The common heritage*

Ballets from the past, referred to here as *traditional* ballets, represent a significant aspect of the cultural heritage of dance as art: *Giselle* (1841), for example, is a symbol of the *Romantic* ballet period and *Swan Lake* (1895) is representative of a typical late nineteenth-century Petipa-style ballet.*

*For source material on Romantic and Petipa-style ballets, see Guest 1966, Roslavleva 1966.

To the iconoclast, traditional ballets might be viewed as museum pieces with little relevance in the context of the fast-moving world of dance as a theatre art today. Compared with the seemingly limitless possibilities of movement invention and the creation of new dance forms through the idiom of modern dance, these ballets might appear anachronistic and stereotyped. To the classicists, however, the perpetuation of these works is important for a variety of reasons: their re-creation enables historical links with the past to be maintained and, through performance, twentieth century audiences are brought in contact with the living tradition of classical ballet. The popularity of *Giselle* is apparent in companies throughout the world and is an indication that this universal theme, sustained for nearly two centuries, remains significant today. Ballets such as *Swan Lake* (1895), *The Sleeping Beauty* (1890) and *Nutcracker* (1892) are an inheritance from a period which placed great emphasis on spectacular virtuoso productions as part of its artistic credo. Petipa-style ballets are structured to incorporate large numbers of dancers from corps-de-ballet up to principal dancers, thus providing dancers with experience in a variety of roles. A further attraction of traditional ballets is that they provide a framework in which companies can display their distinctive identity as well as providing some of the most challenging roles for artistic interpretations by their dancers.

It is not without significance that in the same way that people enjoy a Beethoven symphony or a Shakespearian tragedy, present-day audiences continue to be stimulated by the different qualities which individual dancers bring to well-known roles such as Giselle and Odette/Odile in *Swan Lake*. Ballets such as these represent an important aspect of an historical tradition which is shared by many companies in different parts of the world, and as such, provide a context in which the development of dance as a theatre art in the twentieth century can be studied.

7.2.2 *A unique contribution*

It is possible to point to a number of examples of choreographers in various historical periods who have been instrumental in the establishment of indigenous ballet companies in many parts of the world: Roland Petit in France, Van Manen in Holland, Cranko in Germany, and Ashton in England are some of those who have been influential in the European development of classical ballet in the twentieth century. Each has created works which have contributed uniquely to the choreographic style of individual companies and, in some cases, these ballets have become key works in the establishment of that company's artistic tradition.

Ashton's *Symphonic Variations* created for the then Sadler's Wells Ballet in 1946 is an example of a uniquely English ballet which has never been performed by another company. The work was a significant milestone in Ashton's career as a choreographer and represented an important contribution to the early development of the company (Vaughan 1977, Bland 1981a). The ballet was originally choreographed for Margot Fonteyn, Pamela May, Moira Shearer, Michael Somes, Henry Danton and Brian Shaw, and it is probable that it was an ideal work for the particular qualities of these dancers. Bland (1981a) indicates that *Symphonic Variations* contributed greatly to the success of the Sadler's Wells Company in its first season at Covent Garden. It is generally agreed by historians and critics that *Symphonic Variations*, which is described by Vaughan (1977) as 'The Royal Ballet's signature work', is a work of considerable artistic merit. It is further described by Bland (1981a) as a 'distillation of the English style' and

> one of Ashton's greatest achievements, destined to occupy a unique place in his choreographic repertoire and also in the history of the Royal Ballet.

Since its first staging on 24 April 1946, the ballet has remained in the repertory of the Royal Ballet Company and, according to Bland, the work was performed 144 times between 1946 and 1979.

7.2.3 *Contemporary ballets*

Contemporary ballets are new works created in the classical ballet idiom. Most large-scale ballet companies include new ballets in their repertory and from time to time works are commissioned from choreographers both within and outside the company. Though new works may represent only a small proportion of a ballet company's repertory in any one season, they are significant, in that they enable dancers to extend their experience into new dimensions and provide fresh creative opportunities for choreographers.

Currently there are a number of choreographers working in the field of classical ballet who have established less conventional approaches to choreography. The Dutch choreographer Van Manen is an example of a choreographer who, in some of his works, focuses attention on the choreographic potential of classical ballet as a dance form without direct reference to any narrative or thematic plot. Two of his works created for The Netherlands Dance Theatre, *Grosse Fuge* (1971) and *Septet Extra* (1973), were both revived for Royal Ballet New Group in 1972 and 1974 respectively. Glen Tetley is a further example of a choreographer who is known for his work both in the contemporary dance and classical ballet. Tetley's ballet *Field Figures* was created for the Royal Ballet New Group in 1970 and is described by Bland (1981a) as 'revolutionary' by Royal Ballet standards. An interesting example of a work which reflects new departures for the Royal Ballet Company is the contemporary choreographer Robert North's *Troy Game* which was first presented by the Company on 29 April 1980. *Troy Game* was the first ballet from a contemporary dance company (London Contemporary Dance Theatre) to be taken into the Royal Ballet repertory.

Not all new works are of a 'pioneering' nature. The Royal Ballet's new repertory piece in 1976, for example, was Ashton's *A Month in the Country*, based on Turgenev's literary theme. Corder's *L'Invitation au voyage* is a recent example of a new short ballet by a young choreogapher. It is probable, therefore, that an analysis of the repertory of the Royal Ballet in any one historical period, would reveal a variety of types of new ballets from which possible characterisations could be made.

7.2.4 *Ballet revivals*

Unlike a painting or a sculpture which may have survived the vicissitudes of time intact, ballets from the past cannot be preserved easily. Due to the lack of original sources, the accurate revival of ballets created in the past is fairly tenuous. Even if it were possible to reconstruct such works of art in every detail, it is doubtful if the conventions of the period in which they first originated would appeal to contemporary audiences. Frequently, the musical score remains the only surviving source and even this may be adapted to meet the requirements of a 'modern' production. Despite the existence of several notation systems, the number of ballets which have actually been recorded is few. However, Ann Hutchinson Guest's reconstruction of the pas de six from *La Vivandière* for Sadler's Wells Royal Ballet in 1982 is an example of a recent revival which was made possible by the existence of an original notated score, recorded by the choreographer Arthur Saint-Léon (1848) and transcribed into Labanotation by the reconstructor (Hutchinson Guest 1982). There are a variety of ways in which ballets can be recorded today. The Benesh and Labanotation systems provide the means for dances to be written down and the wider use of film and video techniques also ensures that some ballets which might otherwise be lost are recorded in performance. There is, for example, a film version of Ashton's *Marguerite and Armand*. It is significant that this work, which was created for Fonteyn and Nureyev in 1963, has never been performed by other dancers.

The primary way in which ballets survive, however, is through performance and it is in the tradition of classical ballet as a performing art for ballets to be passed on from one generation of dancers to the next. Alicia Markova, for example, is highly acclaimed for her interpretation of *Les Sylphides* and in the following contextual account, taken from a programme note of her production of *Les Sylphides* for London Festival Ballet (1976), she describes how she came to inherit the role.

> I first danced in *Les Sylphides* with Diaghilev, then with the Vic–Wells Ballet when I staged their first production and afterwards with many other companies throughout the world. But though my performances seemed to satisfy audiences and critics, they never satisfied me. I never really enjoyed *Les Sylphides*. Then, in 1941, came a revelation. I joined the American Ballet Theater and for the first time worked in *Les Sylphides* with its creator, Mikhail Fokine. It was as though a thick curtain had been lifted: I saw the ballet clearly for the first time. Fokine was superb at explanation. Quiet, rather bald and unlike the popular conception of a ballet master, in words and dance he made the ballet come alive as it had never done for me before. He said of one exit, and in a sentence that somehow catches the very essence of *Les Sylphides*, 'You must not simply stand and put your hands above your head: you are reaching for the moon.'

Markova's important link with this ballet was further underlined in B.B.C. Television's *Dance Month 1980* when, as part of a series of master classes, she coached Margaret Barbieri and David Ashmole of the Royal Ballet in the leading roles.

Thus, ballets are perpetuated through revival and unbroken tradition and it is probable that works which are in the repertory of more than one company have a better chance of survival than ballets which remain unique to one company. Ashton's ballet *Façade*, for example, has been in the repertories of several companies. The ballet was first produced for the Camargo Society in 1931, was later taken into the repertory of the Ballet Rambert and in 1935 was revived for the Vic–Wells Ballet. Until recently, the ballet has been maintained in the repertory of the Royal Ballet and has also been revived for several other companies abroad (Vaughan 1977). Nijinska's *Les Noces* is also an example of a ballet with an interesting cultural history. First performed by the Ballets Russes in 1923, it has since been revived for a number of European ballet companies including the Royal Ballet 1966, the Stuttgart Ballet 1974 and the Paris Opera 1976.

7.3 *Choreography based on Shakespearian themes with particular reference to Romeo and Juliet*

Before ballet was performed in public theatres, dances were being made and performed in spectacular settings as part of the European concept of *ballet de cour*. It is generally recognised by historians that choreographers emerged as artists in their own right with the development of *ballet d'action* from the eighteenth century. Since then, choreographers have sought inspiration from a wide range of musical, poetic and literary sources and Shakespearian themes provide one literary source which has featured significantly for many centuries. In the twentieth century several of Shakespeare's themes have been used by choreographers: *A Midsummer Night's Dream* is the basis of Ashton's ballet *The Dream* (1964), Cranko's *Taming of the Shrew* (1969) follows the play of the same title, and *The Tempest* has recently been explored both in the contemporary dance idiom by Tetley (1979) and in the classical style by Nureyev (1982).

Attention is given here to one particular Shakespearian play which has been widely exploited by choreographers in this century, i.e. *Romeo and Juliet*. Bland (1981b) describes *Romeo and Juliet* as

becoming the *Swan Lake* of our time: no self-respecting

classical company can hold up its head without it, and alternative productions spring up like mushrooms.

Historians cite Galeotti's version (1811) with music by Schall as being the earliest documented *Romeo and Juliet,* though Koegler (1977) refers to a previous version choreographed by Luzzi in 1785. The section at the end of this chapter lists some of the known versions of *Romeo and Juliet* and reflects the wide variety of productions in our own century. The list is not exhaustive, however, since it does not include ballets which have been produced for film and television, nor does it take account of the dance elements which exist in operas based on *Romeo and Juliet,* or the definitive work itself, i.e. Shakespeare's play (see Brissenden 1982).

7.3.1 *Romeo and Juliet* – musical scores

There is no definitive scenario or musical score for *Romeo and Juliet.* This is in contrast to a ballet such as *Giselle* which, despite changes in choreography, costumes and sets, remains a two-act ballet based on a libretto by Saint-Georges to the music of Adolphe Adam. The Tchaikovsky score, first produced in the early 1870s, has been used for a high proportion of one-act twentieth century productions of *Romeo and Juliet.* There are also versions to the music of Berlioz, while Tudor's ballet is set to an arrangement of Delius' music by Antal Dorati. The Prokofiev score of *Romeo and Juliet* accounts for the largest number of productions in this century and, since its first performance in Brno, Czechoslovakia with choreography by Psota in 1938, it has been an inspiration to choreographers in many parts of the world. There is a variety of written material on Prokofiev's *Romeo and Juliet* including reports on the circumstances in which the ballet score originated and the composer's collaboration with Lavrovsky culminating in the first Soviet production performed in the Kirov Theatre, Leningrad, in 1940 (Anon. 1965a, Balanchine and Mason 1978, Guest 1975). This is not the place for any detailed discussion, but if, as suggested by Bland (1981b), *Romeo and Juliet* is proving to be the classic ballet of this century, then history might show that the various versions of the ballet owe as much to Prokofiev as to Shakespeare.

7.3.2 *Romeo and Juliet* – choreographic treatment

The theme of Shakespeare's *Romeo and Juliet* has been widely explored in a variety of ballet forms from elaborate full-length works to shorter ballets. It might be predicted, therefore, that the choreographic treatment of Shakespeare's *Romeo and Juliet* has been diverse. The Lavrovsky (1940) version, for example, follows Shakespeare's story fairly closely, while the other Russian version, choreographed by Nijinska for the Ballets Russes in 1929 to the music of Constant Lambert, was based on the story of two lovers eloping while rehearsing for *Romeo and Juliet*. Tudor's ballet, first performed in an incomplete form in New York in 1943 and described by Balanchine and Mason (1978) as a 'dramatic ballet which compresses into one vivid act the tragic love story of Romeo and Juliet', is a further well-documented example (Chujoy 1967, Koegler 1977).

In Section 7.5 at the end of this chapter further details are given of some of the other ballet versions of *Romeo and Juliet* which have been documented, though more information exists which could be located. There is, for example, evidence of other Soviet versions which are not listed. Reference is made in an article by Pitt (1976) to 'recent Soviet versions of *Romeo and Juliet*' which 'have reacted in some way against Lavrovsky's model'. Pitt describes the Vinogradov version for the Maly company in which, she says, he

> has over-simplified by treating the work as a socio-political tract, with the powerful, violent and un-comprehending 'aristos' spoiling the loves and lives of a shining white young couple, who are vaguely upheld by the rather anonymous and shadowy 'People'.

Balanchine and Mason (1978) provide a useful summary of five other interpretations of *Romeo and Juliet* to Prokofiev's score. These are the Lavrovsky version, first presented at the Kirov State Theatre of Opera and Ballet, Leningrad, 11 January 1940; Ashton's version for the Royal Danish Ballet, first performed at the Royal Theatre, Copenhagen, 19 May 1955; Cranko's, first staged for La Scala Opera Ballet at the Teatro Verde, in Venice, 26 July 1958; MacMillan's, first presented by the Royal Ballet at the Royal Opera House, London, 9 February 1965 and, a more recent production by John Neumeier for the Royal Danish Ballet, first performed at the Royal Theatre, Copenhagen, 20 December 1974. All five works have been presented in New York and three, Lavrovsky's, Cranko's and MacMillan's, have been performed in London.

7.4 *MacMillan's Romeo and Juliet*

This section is divided into:

7.4.1 The historical significance of MacMillan's *Romeo and Juliet*

7.4.2 The thematic structure of MacMillan's *Romeo and Juliet*

7.4.3 MacMillan's treatment of the *Romeo and Juliet* theme with reference to other versions

7.4.4 Selected critical reviews of MacMillan's *Romeo and Juliet* 1965–69

7.4.1 *The historical significance of MacMillan's Romeo and Juliet*

Romeo and Juliet: Ballet in three acts
Music: Serge Prokofiev
Choreography: Kenneth MacMillan
Scenery and costumes: Nicholas Georgiadis
Lighting: William Bundy
First performed by the Royal Ballet at the Royal Opera House, Covent Garden on 9 February 1965.

CAST:		
	Juliet	Margot Fonteyn
	Romeo	Rudolf Nureyev
	Mercutio	David Blair
	Tybalt	Desmond Doyle
	Benvolio	Anthony Dowell
	Paris	Derek Rencher
	Lord Capulet	Michael Somes
	Lady Capulet	Julia Farron
	Escalus	Leslie Edwards
	Rosaline	Georgina Parkinson
	Nurse	Gerd Larson
	Friar Lawrence	Ronald Hynd
	Lord Montagu	Franklin White
	Lady Montagu	Betty Kavanagh
	Juliet's Friends	Ann Howard, Carole Hill, Ann Jenner, Jennifer Penney, Diane Horsham, Virginia Wakelyn
	Three Harlots	Deanne Bergsma, Monica Mason, Carole Needham
	Mandolin Dance	Keith Rosson with Robert Mead, Kenneth Mason, Ian Hamilton, Austin Bennett, Lambert Cox

128

The reputation of Kenneth MacMillan's *Romeo and Juliet*, as indicated by Bland (1981a) in his history of the Royal Ballet, is assured. The work, which is the third interpretation of the Prokofiev score by an English choreographer, was first presented in February 1965 at the Royal Opera House, Covent Garden, London, and 'scored a huge success, receiving 43 curtain calls, described in the press as setting some kind of record' (Bland 1981a). Since then the ballet has been presented in its entirety 193 times at Covent Garden and 157 times abroad. Nearly a year after the ballet was premiered in London, Monahan and Clarke (1966) write:

> though very dramatic, it dances, abundantly; though closely tied to Shakespeare and Prokofiev, it allows scope, to an extent almost unique in choreography, for differences in interpretation by numerous Romeos and, especially, Juliets. And, here is its particular unintended, miracle; it has so spotlighted the Romeos, and even more, the Juliets that everyone has been made freshly aware of the rivalry in excellence among the company's up-and-coming leaders. This season, at least, we have been reminded that this is just what the Royal Ballet needs to reinvigorate public interest in it. *Romeo and Juliet* has been, unwittingly, a miracle of timing.

Here Monahan and Clarke highlight the significance of this ballet within the context of the history of the Royal Ballet. At the time the Royal Ballet was under the directorship of Frederick Ashton who had himself produced a version of *Romeo and Juliet* for the Royal Danish Ballet in 1955 but doubted the suitability of this work for a larger company. The repertory, however, needed a major new substantial work as a New York tour was imminent. The company at that time possessed a number of superb dancers including the famous Fonteyn/Nureyev partnership. Although MacMillan created his *Romeo and Juliet* for Lynn Seymour and Christopher Gable, the title roles were danced on the opening night by Fonteyn and Nureyev. The resulting commercial success of the ballet at that time therefore could be judged to be as much Fonteyn's and Nureyev's as MacMillan's and it is interesting that for subsequent performances Covent Garden charged higher prices for performances danced by this famous couple (see Bland 1981a). This practice was later dropped, indicating the potential of the ballet as a vehicle for the interpretations of many other dancers.

The making of *Romeo and Juliet* represented a significant milestone in MacMillan's career. MacMillan was by this time an established choreographer with several ballets to his name (such as *The Invitation*), but this was his first attempt at a full-length work. The critics speculated as to his ability to sustain a full-length work and Monahan (1965a) described him as a choreographer of 'exquisite flashes' rather than 'sustained architecture', though he went on to add that in *Romeo and Juliet* 'he has shown that he can cope with a big canvas'.

There is evidence that MacMillan was particularly attracted to the idea of making a ballet on the theme of Romeo and Juliet (Bland 1981a, Crisp 1965). The Prokofiev score appealed to him and he had been influenced by the Lavrovsky and Cranko versions. He especially admired the latter, created for the Stuttgart Company in 1962. The Lavrovsky version, presented by the Bolshoi Company in London in 1958, had been much acclaimed and it was inevitable that MacMillan's would be compared with it. Monahan (1965a) in his review of the premiere of MacMillan's *Romeo and Juliet* puts forward the view that

> in the inevitable comparison with the Bolshoi production this one suffers in the matter of sheer size. MacMillan's Verona does seem rather sparsely populated when set against Lavrovsky's.

but he goes on to add that

> this is, perhaps, a price that had to be paid for MacMillan's greater (and very welcome) provision of dance

An article by Crisp (1965), based on an interview with MacMillan during the making of the ballet, is an invaluable source of information. The article describes the way in which the ballet was structured and also provides insights into the choreographer's treatment of Shakespeare's theme. MacMillan was faced with an enormous task when creating his first major full-length work. In addition to this new ballet, the Company were also involved in considerable rehearsal schedules for the current repertory and this clearly has some bearing on the way in which MacMillan organised work on the various dances for his *Romeo and Juliet*.

7.4.2 *The thematic structure of MacMillan's Romeo and Juliet*

The action of MacMillan's ballet takes place in three acts made up of 6 scenes in Act 1; 3 scenes in Act 2; 4 scenes in Act 3. The diagram gives an indication of the way in which the ballet is structured, the various scenes within each act and the main components contained therein. As indicated in the diagram, MacMillan choreographed four pas de deux for Juliet: two with Romeo and two with Paris. Those with Romeo are identified as the *2nd and 3rd pas de deux* in Act 1, Scene 6 and Act 3, Scene 1, and those with Paris are the *1st and 4th pas de deux* in Act 1, Scene 4 and in Act 3, Scene 3. For girl soloists there are parts for Rosaline, who features in Act 1, Scene 1 as Romeo's first love, and there are also roles for three Harlots who appear in the 1st, 3rd and 4th Street Scenes set in the Market Place in Verona in Acts 1 and 2. There are also two dances for Juliet's 'six friends', the first in the ballroom, Act 1, Scene 4, and the second in the Flower Dance in Act 3, Scene 3 in Juliet's bedroom. The Family Scenes with Juliet's parents, the Capulets, the Nurse and Paris take place in three scenes in Act 1, Scene 2 and Act 3, Scenes 1 and 3.

There are four major roles for male dancers: Romeo, a Montagu; Mercutio and Benvolio, friends of Romeo; Tybalt, a Capulet cousin. Friar Lawrence does not have a major dancing role and appears in Act 2, Scene 2 and Act 3, Scene 2 only.

According to Crisp (1965), MacMillan feels that, apart from the role of the heroine, *Romeo and Juliet* is 'a man's ballet' and 'has stretched his male dancers to an unusual degree':

> the roles are technically difficult and cover the whole range of the masculine steps (with the exception of double tours en l'air which he thinks are cliches) and for the first time he is using entrechats: Romeo, Mercutio and Benvolio perform one entrechat six.

MacMillan also sees Mercutio, Romeo and Benvolio as 'typical fun-loving youths'. This is exemplified in the vigorous pas de trois which they perform in Act 1, Scene 3 outside the Capulet's house before gate-crashing the ball. MacMillan has created a demanding role for Romeo who, he believes, 'has more dancing than in any other production he has seen' (Crisp 1965). In contrast to Juliet, who is seen purely within the context of her sheltered family background, Romeo is featured as a provocative member of the male-dominated ruling classes. This element is reflected in MacMillan's choreography of the Street Scenes (Act 1, Scene 1, and Act 2, Scene 3) in which interaction between the rival Montagus and Capulets results in brawls and duelling clashes. The action which takes place in the three Street Scenes in Act 1, Scene 1 and Act 2, Scenes 1 and 3 incorporates choreography for the corps de ballet. MacMillan's major choreographic contribution for the corps de ballet, however, is in the Ballroom Scene in Act 1, Scene 4 in which the dancers perform a stately formal dance. It is of interest that here as in other parts of the ballet the corps de ballet wear heeled character shoes in contrast to Juliet and her 'six friends' who dance *en pointe*. The ballroom scene also includes a pas de deux between Juliet and Paris and the 'Mandolin Dance'.

7.4.3 *MacMillan's treatment of the Romeo and Juliet theme with reference to other versions*

As in other versions, notably Lavrovsky's and Cranko's, MacMillan follows Shakespeare and sets his love story in Verona, against the wider social context of the Italian Renaissance evoked in Georgiadis' costumes and sets. Geogiadis' designs,* though not specifically dealt with here, have received much attention in critics' reviews of the ballet and have been compared with those of Pyotr Williams for Lavrovsky and Jurgen Rose for Cranko.

To Crisp (1965) 'it is significant' that MacMillan 'finds an important key to the dramatic action in the family backgrounds of his hero and heroine.' The fate of the two lovers, which is the main motivation in MacMillan's ballet, is seen amidst the background of the rival Montagu and Capulet families. The resulting devastation brought about by the two feuding factions is established in Act 1, Scene 1, which opens in the Market Place and centres on a quarrel between Lady Capulet's nephew Tybalt and Romeo, a Montagu. This is brought to a climax in Act 2, Scene 3, when Romeo avenges the death of his friend Mercutio by killing Tybalt and is exiled. Thus, MacMillan's Street Scenes depict a society, described in Crisp's article as 'violent' and 'patriarchal' and Verona's market

---

*Georgiadis' designs for MacMillan's *Romeo and Juliet* are discussed by Crichton (1965).

Act	Scene	Setting	Action
I	1	Market place	1st street scene; Romeo declares love for Rosaline; Romeo joins Mercutio and Benvolio; Dances for 3 Harlots; Romeo/Tybalt quarrel; Fight between Montagus/Capulets; Prince of Verona orders cease feuding
I	2	Juliet's anteroom	Juliet's first entrance; Playful action with doll; 1st entrance Nurse/Parents/Paris
I	3	Outside Capulet's house	Guests arriving for Ball; *Pas de trois* Romeo/Mercutio/Benvolio; Follows Rosaline to Ball
I	4	Ballroom	Stately dance for corps-de-ballet; *1st pas de deux* Romeo/Juliet/Paris; Romeo Juliet meet; Mandolin dance; 1st dance for Juliet's 'six friends'
I	5	Outside Capulet's house	Guests depart; Tybalt restrained by Lord Capulet from pursuing Romeo
I	6	Balcony scene	*2nd pas de deux* Juliet/Romeo
II	1	Market place	2nd street scene; Wedding procession passes; Romeo receives note from Juliet via Nurse arranging meeting at Friar Lawrence chapel
II	2	Chapel	Secret marriage of Juliet to Romeo
II	3	Market place	3rd street scene; Climax to Capulet/Montagu feud: Tybalt kills Mercutio, Romeo kills Tybalt; Romeo exiled; Lady Capulet grieves Tybalt's death
III	1	Juliet's bedroom	*3rd pas de deux* Juliet/Romeo; 2nd entrance Nurse/Parents/Paris; Juliet's impassioned rejection of Paris
III	2	Chapel	Friar Lawrence gives Juliet the phial of sleeping potion
III	3	Juliet's bedroom	3rd entrance Nurse/Parents/Paris; *4th pas de deux* Juliet/Paris; Bridal flower dance; 2nd dance for Juliet's 'six friends'
III	4	Crypt	Mourners depart; Paris stays and is killed by Romeo; Romeo/Juliet die

place provides a colourful background to the dramatic events which centre on the warring activities of the Montagus and Capulets.

From Crisp's article (1965) it is apparent that in his Ballroom Scene (Act 1, Scene 4) MacMillan intended to present a formal choreographic 'cameo' of a patriarchal society consistent with his less orderly rollicking Street Scenes. This is a reversal of the Lavrovsky interpretation of the Ballroom Scene in which the 'Cushion Dance' might be viewed as a symbol of man subservient to woman. Such diverse interpretations highlight the fact that individual choreographers have interpreted this scene in a variety of ways. The Ballroom Scene is significant in the plot because it provides the background for Romeo and Juliet's first encounter.

In addition to the Lavrovsky 'Cushion Dance' already quoted, Vaughan (1977) points to the Petipa influence which is reflected in Ashton's formal ensembles in his Ballroom Scene. Balanchine and Mason (1978) offer written descriptions of several other versions and although these are undetailed, combined with other evidence, they would provide the basis for a comparative study of the Ballroom Scenes.

Crisp explains that MacMillan's

> rooting of the tragedy within the context of the family and the society is very important as a basis for his work. He sees the Capulets seeking to marry Juliet to Paris for reasons of wealth and aristocratic position

and views Juliet as a

> victim of the attitudes of her parents: for a girl of 14 she is tremendously strong-willed and passionate and takes much of the initiative in the relationship with Romeo.
>
> (1965)

The domestic side of MacMillan's ballet is depicted in three scenes in Acts 1 and 3. On each of these occasions MacMillan has formalised the action in a way that

> seems to underline, as did the stately dancing at the ball, an adult rigidity which was a part of behaviour in those times.
>
> (Williams et al, 1966)

The scenes follow a pattern which is characterised as

> a procession of nurse, mother, father, and suitor – always coming through the same door to almost identical music and always expressing concern in almost identical gestures.
>
> (Williams *et al* 1966)

A further significant aspect of these scenes is that Juliet has a meeting with Paris, her suitor, in Act 1, Scene 2, prior to the ball in Act 1, Scene 4. This is a departure from the Lavrovsky and Cranko versions in which Juliet does not meet Paris until the ballroom scene. In these cases, Juliet's rejection of Paris might, therefore, be understood in the light of her love at first sight for Romeo. In MacMillan's version, however, Juliet's sudden attachment to Romeo in the Ballroom Scene could be seen as more credible in the knowledge of her previous lack of interest in Paris at their first meeting. Juliet's positive attitude in this respect is further demonstrated in Act 2, Scene 1 when she precipitates her marriage to Romeo by sending him a letter via her nurse arranging a meeting at Friar Lawrence's chapel.

In Romeo, MacMillan portrays a fun-loving youth who at the beginning is in love with Rosaline. It is not, therefore, surprising that MacMillan, like Cranko, focuses attention on the interaction between Romeo and Rosaline in the first act of the ballet. In the first scene 'Romeo tries to declare his love for the lovely Rosaline who rejects him.' (Balanchine and Mason 1978). MacMillan, again like Cranko, uses Rosaline as a device for enticing Romeo to the Capulet ball, a point which is taken up by Monahan (1965a):

> Romeo's first glimpse of Juliet at the Capulet ball is made all blurred and inconsiderable by the fact, that after Juliet's rightly conspicuous entry, Romeo remains attentive to Rosaline.

In Tybalt MacMillan established a strong character who, he feels,

> wants to dominate the Capulet household and assume the position of father

and MacMillan is further

> intrigued by the character of Lady Capulet and by the
> extent of her grief at Tybalt's death since he is, after all,
> only her nephew
>
> (Crisp 1965)

It is, therefore, not without significance that at the end of Act 2,
Scene 3

> Lady Capulet holds the body of her nephew, swaying
> back and forth in her grief as her husband watches
> helplessly.
>
> (Balanchine and Mason 1978)

Though it is probable that MacMillan intended to point to deeper
psychological undertones in the relationship between Tybalt and
Lady Capulet, this aspect of his interpretation appears to have
caused consternation among some critics. Williams *et al* (1966), for
example, are critical of MacMillan's 'understanding of aristocratic
behaviour in the Renaissance' which they intimate is better handled
in the Lavrovsky version. It does not seem credible that

> however overwhelmed with grief when her nephew
> Tybalt is slaughtered at the end of the second act, that
> Lady Capulet would roll about in the dirt.

Whatever the merits or demerits of the more obscure domestic elements of MacMillan's *Romeo and Juliet*, in his treatment of the
relationship between hero and heroine he has created a powerful
evocation of Shakespeare's tragedy. MacMillan's 'ecstatic'
choreography of the pas de deux for Juliet and Romeo in the
Balcony and Bedroom Scenes is sharply contrasted to the more
formal and reserved dancing between Juliet and Paris in the
Ballroom Scene and later in Act 3. The balcony pas de deux in
which Romeo and Juliet declare their eternal love ends the first act
of the ballet. Significantly, it is the only scene in which Romeo and
Juliet remain the sole characters on stage throughout, and, as such,
represents a dramatic focal point in the ballet. Thus, in contrast to
the elaborate and opulent atmosphere created in many of the other
scenes, the balcony pas de deux focuses attention entirely on the
lovers themselves. The second pas de deux in Act 3, Juliet's
bedroom, which might be interpreted as a symbolic consummation

136

of their mutual love, is contrasted in the same scene by her impassioned rejection of Paris. This leads her, in Act 3, Scene 3, to drink the sleeping potion given to her by Friar Lawrence which results in death-like sleep. In the final scene of the ballet, with Paris dead and the mourners departed, MacMillan again centres the dramatic action on the tragic circumstances of the hero and heroine. Unlike Lavrovsky, who, following Shakespeare, ends his ballet with the reconciliation of the Montagus and Capulets, MacMillan, like Ashton and Cranko, finalises his tragedy with the death of the two lovers in the crypt.

7.4.4 *Selected critical reviews of MacMillan's Romeo and Juliet, 1965–69*

Following the world premiere of MacMillan's *Romeo and Juliet* the notices were wide-ranging. A *Dancing Times* article, 'What the papers said about *Romeo and Juliet*', (Anon. 1965b) gives an interesting selection of the various critical reviews which appeared in many of the newspapers and includes: Alexander Bland, *The Observer*; Richard Buckle, *The Sunday Times*; A. V. Coton, *The Daily Telegraph*; James Monahan, *The Guardian*; Andrew Porter, *The Financial Times*. The following is a cross-section of extracts from these reviews –

> MacMillan's intimate scenes are lovely;
> the crowd scenes are tame and conventional,
> the fighting dull.   (*The Sunday Times*)

> MacMillan has found the known repertory of classical
> and romantic movement adequate to his expressive ends.
>   (*Financial Times*)

> MacMillan has succeeded notably in the psychological
> insight he offers into Juliet, his conception of Romeo as a
> roarin' Renaissance boy, and certain passages of his
> pure dance choreography which match Ashton in
> Copenhagen, and leave the rest of the field standing.
>   (*The Times*)

> The scenery, frequently and adroitly changed, is always
> gorgeous and the costumes are a tasteful, uncumbersome
> evocation of Ghirlandaio.
>   (*The Guardian*)

Since 1965 MacMillan's ballet has been performed many times with different casts and in various parts of the world. The successful impact of the ballet following its London premiere was carried over in the following spring when the Royal Ballet Company performed their New York season. Moore (1965) described the ballet as 'an absolute smash hit'. In her article Moore also hints at comparisons between MacMillan's *Romeo and Juliet* and other versions seen in New York; these are Lavrovsky's, Ashton's and Tudor's. She points to the merits of MacMillan's choreography:

> in the stylized but masterful handling of the crowd scenes, the ensembles in the ballroom, in memorable bits of characterization, and in the splendid opportunities offered by the two roles which, after all, must provide the point and focus of the entire ballet.

A few years later, in 1969, following MacMillan's revival of his *Romeo and Juliet* for the Royal Swedish Ballet, Percival (1970) reviews the ballet in a fresh context. His observations are significant in that they provide points of contrast between the two companies, Royal Ballet and Royal Swedish, and their individual interpretations. Percival clearly admired the Stockholm production and highlights certain material advantages which he feels enhance the presentation. He compares the orchestra favourably, for example, with that at Covent Garden and indicates that the shape of the stage results 'in the interior and exterior scenes gaining in realism'. He also remarks that

> the Stockholm workshops have taken some trouble to make things look right – the market scene reveals credible joints of meat for sale, rather than the clumsy, solid, un-prepossessing carcass lugged about at Covent Garden, which is so stiff that one imagines Verona must have imported frozen Argentine beef.

Percival is similarly impressed by some of the revisions to Georgiadis' costume designs: Romeo's 'first entry in white', for example, enables him to 'stand out' from the start. Percival's observations on some of the role interpretations are also revealing. In the case of Lady Capulet, danced by Viveka Ljung, he finds a more credible mother to Juliet.

The relationship between different casts and interpretation of roles is a significant aspect of the historical development of any ballet. In the case of MacMillan's *Romeo and Juliet*, which has been presented by two companies, the number of alternative casts rises dramatically. From the outset the interpretations of MacMillan's characters, in particular those of Juliet and Romeo, have caused considerable interest among critics. As previously indicated, MacMillan choreographed his Juliet and Romeo on Seymour and Gable, though the ballet was premiered by Fonteyn and Nureyev. Other couples, however, such as Park and MacLeary and Sibley and Dowell, were also instrumental in establishing the ballet. Following the opening night, with Fonteyn and Nureyev, the critic for *The Financial Times* wrote

> Now Juliet is plainly a role conceived for Lynn Seymour, and so until we have seen her dance it we cannot be precise about MacMillan's intentions. As interpreted by Fonteyn last night, this Juliet does not grow up in the way that Ulanova and Struchkova did. Nor does Romeo have the Mantuan soliloquy . . . in which, on learning of Juliet's death, he turns suddenly from ardent boy to resolute man

(Anon. 1965b)

Since then the four original Romeos and Juliets have been reviewed in a variety of articles (for example, Clarke 1967, Monahan 1965b, Williams *et al.* 1966). Judging from these articles it is possible to assume that much of the initial impact of MacMillan's *Romeo and Juliet* was attributable to the interpretation of the early soloists. This is amplified by Monahan (1965b), who writes:

> though MacMillan made this ballet for Seymour and Gable and though Fonteyn and Nureyev bestowed a first-night benediction on it, neither have Fonteyn and Nureyev annexed it, nor have Seymour and Gable established a claim to it as inalienably theirs; it has proved to be an astonishing show-piece for no fewer than four Romeos and, especially, four Juliets, all dissimilar, all valid and exciting.

To date, MacMillan's *Romeo and Juliet* was last performed in 1979. The criticisms mentioned here represent only a small proportion of those written in the early period of the ballet. Critics' reviews, it might be assumed, change as a ballet matures and, with the benefit of more prolonged viewing, may gain in objectivity what they lose in spontaneity.

It is of interest to note that since the presentation of the Stuttgart production in London in the 1970s some critics have ventured to draw comparisons between Cranko's and MacMillan's versions. Crabb (1977) is an example:

> Cranko has more dramatic logic, is perhaps closer to Shakespeare, generates enormous excitement in his fights and moves crowds naturally and effortlessly. MacMillan pours his talent into a succession of ravishing pas de deux, occasionally allowing other components to suffer by default. Which one prefers depends on one's priorities.

This statement, though generalised, does present a balanced summary of the two interpretations. It is possible, therefore, that an examination of additional critical reviews over a more extended time scale may offer further insights both into MacMillan's *Romeo and Juliet* and into other versions. Cranko's *Romeo and Juliet* has, for example, recently been taken into the repertory of a British company. The work was created for the Stuttgart Ballet in 1962 and was first performed by Scottish Ballet in 1982. The fact that this work is now in a British repertory makes it more accessible for viewing and also means that written evidence such as programme notes, reviews and articles are generated. In addition, there is much written documentation on Cranko's work with the Stuttgart Company which includes reviews of the *Romeo and Juliet* production performed in London in the 1970s. Such evidence could well form the basis of a comparative study of Cranko's *Romeo and Juliet* with that of MacMillan.

7.5 Examples of C20th ballets based on Shakespeare's Romeo and Juliet

Title	Choreographer	Music	Company	Place	Date	Comments
Romeo et Juliette	Balanchine/Nijinska	Lambert	Diaghilev's Ballets Russes	Monte Carlo	4 May 1926	ballet based on the story of two dancers who elope while rehearsing for *Romeo & Juliet*
Romeo & Juliet	Christensen	Tchaikovsky	San Francisco Ballet	San Francisco	20 April 1938	
Romeo & Juliet	Harangozo	Tchaikovsky	Royal Hungarian Opera	Budapest	19 April 1939	
Romeo & Juliet	Lavrovsky	Prokofiev	1. Kirov Ballet	Leningrad	11 Jan. 1940	3—act work — following Shakespeare
			2. Bolshoi Ballet revival	Moscow	28 Dec. 1946	this version performed at Royal Opera House, London, 3 Oct. 1956
Romeo & Juliet	Psota	Prokofiev	Yugoslav National Ballet of Zagreb	Brno, Czechoslovakia	Dec. 1938	first ballet performance of Prokofiev's score
Romeo & Juliet	Tudor	Delius	1. Ballet Theatre	Metropolitan Opera House, New York	6 April 1943	the ballet was incomplete at this performance
			2. Royal Swedish revival	Royal Opera House, Stockholm	30 Dec 1962	ballet in 1 act – the work was later revived for American Ballet Theatre, 22 July 1971
Romeo & Juliet	Culberg	Prokofiev		Stockholm	1944	
Romeo et Juliette	Lifar	Tchaikovsky	1. Nouveau Ballet de Monte Carlo		1946	originally for debut of Ludmilla Tcherina – Salle Pleyel, Paris, 16 June 1942
			2. Paris Opera revival	Paris	13 April 1949	

7.5 Examples of C20th ballets based on Shakespeare's Romeo and Juliet *cont.*

Title	Choreographer	Music	Company	Place	Date	Comments
Romeo & Juliet	Parlic	Prokofiev	Belgrade Opera Ballet		25 June 1948	Italian performance Florence Teatre della Pergola 13 May 1955
Romeo & Juliet	Gsovsky	Prokofiev	Deutsche Staatsoper Ballet	Germany	1947	
Romeo & Juliet	Froman	Prokofiev	Yugoslav National Ballet	Belgrade	June 1949	first ballet to Prokofiev's score to be performed in London: Stoll Theatre, 26 Jan. 1955
Romeo & Juliet	Bartholin	Tchaikovsky	Royal Danish Ballet	Copenhagen	8 Dec. 1950	re-staging of original version for Ballet de la Jeunesse, Paris 1937
Tragédie à Vérone	Skibine	Tchaikovsky	Grand Ballet du Marquis de Cuevas		4 May 1950	
Romeo & Juliet	Ashton	Prokofiev	Royal Danish Ballet	Copenhagen	19 May 1955	3-act ballet – following Shakespeare. N.Y. premiere 26 Sept. 1956
Romeo & Juliet	Gnatt	Tchaikovsky	New Zealand Ballet	New Zealand	1955	
Romeo & Juliet	Lifar	Prokofiev	Paris Opera		29 Dec. 1955	
Romeo & Juliet	Golovine, Skibine, Skouresterif, Taras	Berlioz	Grand Ballet du Marquis de Cuevas	Paris – courtyard of the Louvre	29 June 1955	pas de deux – performed by Royal Ballet Touring Company 23 Nov. 1972
Romeo & Juliet	Briansky	Tchaikovsky	Tamara Toumanova/Briansky	Peru	December 1956	pas de deux – performed London Festival Hall 1958

Romeo & Juliet	Lazzini	Tchaikovsky	Compagnie du Théatre Royal de Liège	France	1956	
Romeo & Juliet	Bolender	Tchaikovsky	New York Brooklyn Academy of Music Dance/Drama Co.	New York	19 Jan. 1958	
Romeo & Juliet	Cranko	Prokofiev	1. La Scala Opera Ballet 2. Stuttgart Ballet revival	Teatro Verde, Venice Stuttgart	26 July 1958 2 Dec. 1962	3-act work following Shakespeare taken into Scottish Ballet repertory 1982
Romeo & Juliet	Legat	Berlioz/ Tchaikovsky	Legat School	King George's Hall, London	15 Dec. 1962	
Romeo & Juliet	MacMillan	Prokofiev	1. Royal Ballet Company 2. Royal Swedish Ballet revival	London Stockholm	9 Feb 1965 1969	3-act ballet following Shakespeare – N.Y. premiere April 1965
Romeo & Juliet	Youskevitch	Tchaikovsky	Ballet Romantique	N.Y. High School of Printing	6 Feb. 1965	
Romeo & Juliet	Béjart	Berlioz	Ballet of the C20th	Brussels	17 Nov. 1966	modern version
Romeo & Juliet	Beriosoff	Prokofiev	Zurich Stadttheater Ballet	Zurich	19 Nov. 1966	
Romeo & Juliet	Bruhn	Prokofiev	Teatro dell'Opera	Rome	March 1966	pas de deux – performed by American Ballet Theatre 10 May 1967
Romeo & Juliet	Dantzig	Prokofiev	Dutch National Ballet	Amsterdam	22 Feb. 1966	
Romeo & Juliet	Labis	Prokofiev	Paris Opera Ballet	Paris	18 Jan. 1967	

7.5 Examples of C20th ballets based on Shakespeare's Romeo and Juliet *cont.*

Title	Choreographer	Music	Company	Place	Date	Comments
Romeo & Juliet	Page	Tchaikovsky	Ruth Page's International Ballet	Chicago	2 Feb. 1969	first performed Niles, Michigan, 14 Jan. 1969
Romeo & Juliet	Araiz	Prokofiev	Ballet Del Teatro San Martin	Buenos Aires	15 Sept. 1970	performed by Joffrey Ballet N.Y. City Centre, 11 Oct. 1977
Romeo & Juliet	Neumeier	Prokofiev	1. Stadtische Buhnen Ballet	Frankfurt	14 Feb. 1971	3-act ballet following Shakespeare
			2. Royal Danish Ballet	Copenhagen	14 Dec. 1974	N.Y. premiere 20 May 1976
Romeo & Juliet	Petrov	Prokofiev	Pittsburg Ballet Theatre	Pittsburg, Heinz Hall	8 Sept. 1971	
Romeo & Juliet	Walter	Prokofiev	Deutsche Oper am. Rhein	Dusseldorf	9 Jan. 1972	
Romeo & Juliet	Dijk	Prokofiev	Ballet du Rhin	Strasbourg	15 Oct. 1976	
Romeo & Juliet	Smuin	Prokofiev	San Francisco Ballet	San Francisco	27 Jan. 1976	performed Edinburgh Festival 1981
Romeo & Juliet	Nureyev	Prokofiev	London Festival Ballet	London	2 June 1977	3-act ballet following Shakespeare
Romeo & Juliet	Grigorovich	Prokofiev	Paris Opera Ballet	Paris	22 Feb. 1978	
Romeo & Juliet	Jakokiak and Pilato	Prokofiev	Essen Stadttheater	Essen	(fall) 1979	

References

Balanchine, G. & Mason, F. 1978 *Balanchine's festival of ballet*. London: Allen
Bland, A. 1981a *The Royal Ballet: the first 50 years*. London: Threshold
Blasis, C. 1820, 1968 *An elementary treatise upon the theory and practice of the art of dancing*. New York: Dover
Brinson, P. 1966 *Background to European ballet*. Netherlands: Sijthoff-Leyden
Brinson, P. & Crisp, C. 1980 *Ballet and dance: a guide to the repertory*. London: David & Charles
Brissenden, A. 1981 *Shakespeare and the dance*. London: Macmillan
Chujoy, A. 1967 *The dance encyclopedia*. New York: Simon & Schuster
Clarke, M. & Crisp, C. 1981 *The Ballet-goer's guide*. London: Michael Joseph
Guest, I. 1960 *The Dancer's Heritage*. London: A. & C. Black
Guest, I. 1966 *The Romantic ballet in Paris*. London: Pitman
Gulbenkian Foundation 1980 *Dance education and training in Britain*
Koegler, H. 1977 *The concise Oxford dictionary of ballet*. London: O.U.P.
Roslaveva, M. 1966 *Era of the Russian balle*. London: Gollancz
Vaughan, D. 1977 *Frederick Ashton and his ballets*. London: Black

Journals and Newspapers

Anon. March 1965a 'Ulanova remembers' and 'Lavrovsky's tribute', *Dancing Times*
Anon. April 1965b 'What the papers said about *Romeo and Juliet*', *Dancing Times*
Bland, A. 23 August 1981b Review, *The Observer*
Clarke, M. April 1967 'Sibley and Dowell in *Romeo and Juliet*', *Dancing Times*
Clarke, M. January 1983 'Royal Ballet at Covent Garden', *Dancing Times*
Crabb, M. March 1977 'Canadian Silver Jubilee', *Dancing Times*
Crichton, R. April 1965 'Romeo's designer Nicholas Georgiadis', *Dancing Times*
Crisp, C. February 1965 '*Romeo and Juliet* and Kenneth MacMillan', *Dancing Times*
Gow, G. June 1979 'Entente cordiale', *Dancing Times*
Hutchinson Guest, A. March 1982 *Vivandière* for the S.W.R.B., *Dancing Times*
Monahan, J. March 1965a 'MacMillan's *Romeo and Juliet* review of the opening night', *Dancing Times*
Monahan, J. April 1965b 'The other Romeos and Juliets', *Dancing Times*
Monahan, J. & Clarke, M. January 1966 'The return of *Romeo and Juliet*', *Dancing Times*
Moore, L. June 1965 'Furore and fantasy: the Royal Ballet reconquers New York', *Dancing Times*
Percival, J. March 1970 'Fresh air in Verona: MacMillan's *Romeo and Juliet* by the Royal Swedish Ballet', *Dancing Times*
Pitt, F. September 1976 'Festivals in Italy and Paris', *Dancing Times*
Williams, P., Percival, J., Montague, M. & Goodwin, N. January 1966 'Verona revisited', *Dancing Times*

Programme Notes

Guest, I. 26 July 1975 Royal Ballet Production – MacMillan's *Romeo and Juliet*

Markova, A. 1976 London Festival Ballet – Markova production *Les Sylphides*

Additional useful Articles (relating to Cranko's *Romeo and Juliet* not quoted in text)

Clarke, M. May 1982 'Scottish Ballet's *Romeo and Juliet*', *Dancing Times*

Maegraith, M. P. July 1974 'Cranko, his influence, his succession in Stuttgart', *Dancing Times*

Monahan, J. July 1976 'Stuttgart in London', *Dancing Times*

Schaefer, W. E. May 1976 'Cranko in Stuttgart', *Dancing Times*

Williams, P. July 1976 'What makes a company: the Stuttgart Ballet in London and at home', *Dance and Dancers*

Other useful Texts

Crisp, C., Sainsbury, A., Williams, P. (eds.) 1976 *Ballet Rambert: 50 years and on*. London: Scolar

Goodwin, N. 1979 *A ballet for Scotland: the first ten years of the Scottish Ballet*. Edinburgh: Canongate

CHAPTER 8

Early European modern dance

by Michael Huxley

8.1 Early European modern dance: the changing viewpoint
8.2 Studying early European modern dance 1910–33
8.3 The study of modern dance as a distinctive form: approaches and topics

This chapter outlines aspects of the historical study of a dance form through examination of some of the particular problems encountered with *early European modern dance* during the period 1910–33. The subject is examined in terms of: the nature of the topic itself; the methodological problems brought to light by the study of the subject; suggested areas and approaches for historical study.

8.1 *Early European modern dance: the changing viewpoint*

The German dance critic Hans Brandenburg compiled various editions of one of the earliest surveys of modern dance in Europe. His 1921 edition of *Der moderne Tanz* catalogued and reviewed the production of dance in Germany during the preceding decade. He included German dancers such as Mary Wigman; German-based dancers including Rudolf von Laban; American artists working in Europe such as Isadora Duncan; dancers from Russia like Anna Pavlova; the work of many other dancers and of dance schools of various styles. Modern dance appears to have been taken to refer to 'dance of the time' without great regard for artistic distinctions and, in the descriptions of the work of the dance schools, without too great a regard for the making of an art product as such.

A decade later, following Martha Graham's first performances in America, John Martin attempted to characterise what was, from his critic's standpoint, the modern dance. He made it quite clear that in considering dance as a 'fine art' the major distinction was between modern dance on the one hand and classical or romantic ballet on the other, each having 'distinguishing features' (1933, pp. 3–5). However, his stated differences between the work of German modern

147

dancers and their American counterparts were given as a matter of emphasis rather than category.

Maynard took a similar view some thirty years later after the 'burgeoning' of modern dance in America (1965). Her *genealogical* account, using a family tree of influence, attempted to locate common origins for American and European modern dance prior to 1910 by reference to François Delsarte and his theories. The genealogical approach was used again by McDonagh to establish categories of generations of modern dancers (1976). This approach, which has been generally adhered to since, took for its content dancers who were almost exclusively American. This American dominated consensus is further compounded by writers such as Murray: she dismisses early European modern dance in Germany as 'Continental excursions' (1979, p. 81).

McDonagh's revisionist view is somewhat redressed by recent American dance historians such as Cohen (1977) and Brown (1980). They have compiled primary source collections according to generations of modern dancers but both reaffirm the place of Mary Wigman, for instance, and Cohen includes Wigman's seminal essay from 1933, 'The philosophy of modern dance'.

The problem for the dance historian is one of locating when a *consensus* existed, the reasons for it and how these are located in the dance itself, in its components, relationships and meanings. Subsequent accounts may help to locate a period within the form as a whole but often, as shown in McDonagh's case, they may conspire to confuse the reader. This is of particular importance because the topic is usually approached from the standpoint of the current consensus. Taking the view typified by Murray that early European modern dance was a mere 'excursion' might dissuade the reader from further study. It has been shown that this account is at odds with primary sources such as Martin and it is likely that its inaccuracy is derived from errors compounded in secondary sources.

The three ways of describing a form of dance have all been illustrated in this example. The term 'modern dance' has *named* different types of dances at different times. The *consensus* during the period 1920–33 appears to have changed from one that included ballet to one that excluded it but considered 'modern dance' to be a transatlantic phenomenon. The view of modern dance as a whole, and during this period specifically, has given greater or lesser emphasis to this consensus according to the author. Authors of both primary and secondary sources have *identified distinctive concepts* – particularly Martin (1933) and Maynard (1965). Certain other topics are suggested by this example – for instance, the large and diffuse nature of modern dance and the use of genealogical accounts. By looking at one aspect of modern dance certain procedures can be isolated and these, in turn, may be applied to modern dance as a whole.

8.2 *Studying early European modern dance 1910–33*

Chapters 4–6 deal with dance subjects that may be studied according to the type of source material chosen. The following points assume a chosen subject area and, in this case, indicate some examples of sources and their usage.

Availability of source material

The *quantity* and *type* of the more common sources changes noticeably from 1910–33. At the start of the period most published material is in the form of reviews and articles in non-dance periodicals. The number of books relevant to dance in general and modern dance in particular increases markedly throughout this time. The first German specialist dance journal, *Der Tanz*, was published as late as 1927. (This compares with the development of regular journals in England and America – the *Dancing Times* from 1910 and *Dance Magazine* from 1925). A similar situation obtains in the case of film but for different, technical, reasons. Comparatively little theatre dance was filmed prior to 1920, some German dance was recorded during the 1920s but more film was made in America in the 1930s. Film is a rare source compared with later periods of modern dance, and reliance must be placed upon written materials to some extent. Many photographs were taken during this period and books were well illustrated. Technical limitations required that most dance was posed in the studio rather than captured in performance: action photographs were often obtained using daylight conditions out of doors. It would be inaccurate, however, to assume from photographic evidence alone that dance was not performed in the theatre. Some dances from the period were notated in a rudimentary form of what was to develop into Kinetography Laban (Labanotation). Reading these sources requires a historical reinterpretation of the notation system itself from a starting point such as Knust (1979) in comparison with von Laban (1930).

Access to these sources presents further problems. Whereas much of the American material of this period is readily available, a great deal of its European equivalent is not. Four typical reasons may serve to highlight the problem. Firstly, American material is well collected and documented in archives such as the New York Public Library: no comparable compilation exists in Europe for the period. Secondly, some material has limited accessibility: for instance East German archives are not always open to Western dance researchers. Thirdly, much of the German and some of the English material in existence during the period was destroyed or dispersed during World War II. Fourthly, film stock of the period was nitrate-based and this type of film deteriorated drastically with time: some film has been retrieved and copied but much has been lost for ever.

The main lesson to be learnt here is that the limited amount of source material commonly available obscures the extent of sources that were in existence and which may, in many cases, be rediscovered.

Problems associated with translation and cultural differences

It goes without saying that international studies of dance often involve the use of translation. Indeed, the history of ballet with its Italian, French, Danish and Russian sources poses even greater problems for the English speaking reader than does the history of modern dance.

Whenever translated material is used it is usual to regard the translated text as being *akin to a secondary source*. The translator may be regarded as mediating between the original text and the reader and although the material of the text remains a primary source the meaning may be altered by the process of translation. Thus there is a need to take into account the abilities of the translator. In the field of early European modern dance two writers and dance historians are particularly well known – Horst Koegler and Walter Sorell. The following example illustrates how writers such as these have gained a reputation for accuracy. Koegler has written two monographs on dance in Germany during the Weimar period. His first study was written from mainly German sources, in German, for a German publication. When asked to write an English version, he chose to write it in English from the same German sources rather than to translate it. That is to say that being bilingual he was able to write directly about the dance and its meaning rather than merely transposing words from one language to another. Whilst it is not expected that everyone studying in this area has that facility it would be expected that the reliability of a translated source would be tested in a similar manner.

The quantity of translated material may impose limitations on the type of study attempted. For instance, von Laban wrote prolifically during the period 1910–33 but only one of his books appeared in English (1930). His only other book in translation is a biography (1935) and this is not representative of the main body of his German writing which is to be found in the years 1920–30. Of course, subsequent to his arrival in England in 1938 a number of books appeared in English, but these were written in England some twenty-five years after his first German book. The case of von Laban is typical of other dancers and writers of the period. Indeed it is only dance makers of the period such as von Laban and Wigman (e.g. 1975) who have been presented in English. Dance historians and critics such as Brandenburg remain largely untranslated.

There are further considerations, however, in addition to the transposing of the written word, its accuracy and its availability. The structure and use of language is inextricable from its meaning. What is described in Germany as *Tanz* does not necessarily correspond to its direct English translation *dance*. Cultural differences must also be considered. The following example illustrates how dance is culture-bound – that is to say, that the meaning of a particular manifestation of dance may be specific to the place of its origin as well as to its historical location. In Germany during the 1920s many terms were associated with what the Germans described as *moderne Tanz*. Two of these terms cause particular difficulty: *Ausdruckstanz* and *Bewegungskunst*. Koegler makes it clear that *Ausdruckstanz* should be taken to mean 'dance of expression, not expressionist dance' (1974, p. 4). Many English writers from the 1920s onwards have, however, used the latter term loosely in making a witting comparison between modern dance and the artistic genre of Expressionism or, more unfortunately, in making an unwitting comparison. Such an inaccurate account based on the naming of dance should not be confused with considered comparisons between modern dance and Expressionism by writers such as Patterson, where distinctive conceptual similarities are identified (1981). A further common misinterpretation is to use 'expressive' as a translation, a fault made by writers familiar with the related but distinctly different method of teaching 'expressive dance' in English schools. The reasons for this difficulty can be traced to the German language itself. Its structure allows the use of complex nouns to make subtle distinctions between different types of dance whereas in English we tend to make use of transferable adjectives. There is nothing surprising in the use, particularly during this period, of combined German nouns. Words like *Tanzkunst* (dance art) and *Bewegungskunst* (movement art) were appropriate for the era and were related to each other in a manner similar to *Tanzschrift* (dance writing) and *Bewegungschrift* (movement writing) which were subtly different but often interchangeable. When von Laban came to England in 1938 the terms accompanied him. The translation of a word from that earlier period in a different culture was chosen to describe his work – *Bewegungskunst* became 'art of movement'. However in England, unlike Germany, this usage was largely in isolation from the similar, earlier terms. At the same time, in the early 1940s, a new term was coined: 'modern educational dance'. The continuing confusion caused by this choice of a translated German term and the concurrent coining of a new English expression is well illustrated by the many discussions about the differences between 'art of movement' and 'modern educational dance'. The complexities of the assumed distinctions between the two are well shown in Hamby's analysis forty years later (1978).

Problems of translation and cross-cultural differences provide, in themselves, one of the most interesting and challenging fields of dance history.

Interpretation of source material

To reiterate a point made in earlier chapters – sources have to be *interpreted* with a view to the *bias* of the writer before their *value* can be judged. In the light of the previous section the same consideration applies to translators. Such interpretation may be quite complex but the two main considerations that apply are, firstly, the position of the author vis-à-vis the dance and those concerned with dance, and, secondly, the postion of the author and text with regards to the wider historical location.

It may be necessary to evaluate an author's work merely by reference to its historical location within the dance sphere. Such an examination requires, where possible, placing the source in question within the context of its author's other writings in order to establish her/his world view of dance and the place of modern dance within that world view. A major topic in this area is the antipathy towards early European modern dance shown in the bias of ballet critics of the time. Such a bias should be suspected but not taken for granted. For instance, Fernau Hall, writing in 1950 on modern English ballet, appears at first reading to be both knowledgeable about and sympathetic toward what he describes as 'the free dance'. His observations go well beyond the brief appreciation of Jooss typical of contemporary ballet critics such as Haskell. Indeed, Hall goes so far as to detail one European expatriate's work extensively: his book containing one of the most appreciative accounts of the work of Ernest Berk. However, Hall's work is put in perspective when it is understood that his training included not only ballet under Sokolova but also 'modern' with Berk and that he performed with both ballet and modern companies.

Scrutiny of sources in this way not only makes the student aware of bias inherent in critics' writing but also acknowledges the role played by such critics in defining the descriptive and evaluative features of a dance form.

When considering interpretation according to historical location, it is worth re-stating that the first concern of dance history is dance and not history in general. However, the question does arise as to what level of knowledge outside dance is necessary to give an accurate historical account. The following example is given to illustrate the ways in which historical location of source material is necessary.

In this chapter early European modern dance has been placed within the period 1910–33. Of course the dance makers of this period continued to work, often in a recognisably similar way, for some years after 1933. The choice of 1933 to mark the end of this period is not arbitrary, neither does the date refer to a specific dance event: 1933 marks both the end of the Weimar Republic and the seizure of complete political power by the Nazi party in Germany with the establishment of the Third Reich. Other writers use the same dating criterion but choose a period appropriate to the particular art under discussion: thus Willett selects 1917–33 (1978); Patterson (1981), in discussing German theatre, considers 1900–33. The exception is Koegler (1974), but his monograph 'In the shadow of the swastika: dance in Germany, 1927–1936' is specifically con-cerned with chronicling dance in the light of the rise of Nazism. It should not be assumed that, by selecting 1933 as a cut-off date for early European dance, subsequent events are of lesser importance. Rather that political events from 1933 onwards directly impinged on the arts in general and dance in particular, and that the period 1933–39 takes on a particular importance in the light of this knowledge.

A close examination of dance in Germany during the 1920s and 1930s emphasises the direct connection between dance and political change. Two of many manifestations illustrate this point. Firstly, in 1933 and during the subsequent years many artists and dancers fled from Germany: in dance the most prominent example was the emigration of Kurt Jooss, Sigurd Leeder and their entire company and school. Many of these artists and a number of the members of Ballets Jooss, particularly Jooss's composer Fritz Cohen, were Jewish. Secondly, at a more subtle level there appears to be a change in terminology associated with dance in Germany with noticeably less reference to *moderne Tanz* and an increasing concern with *Deutsche Tanz* (German dance). Both these observations require direct reference to specific political changes. In 1935 the Nuremburg Laws and the National Law of Citizenship decreed who was to be excluded from German citizenship thereby formalising the persecution of Jews in particular. Of the many political changes in the arts the most often quoted is the attempted exclusion of modernism from public life which culminated in the Munich 'Exhibition of Degenerate Art' in 1937. The vilification of the artists of the modern school from all over Europe including Dix, Kokoschka, Kandinsky and Mondrian, was contrasted with the adulation of ideologically 'pure' work in the accompanying 'First Exhibition of German Art'.

The Nazi search for racial purity included not only the artist but also the art work itself. The change in naming, from *modern* to *German* dance is consistent with the changes in the other arts. Having identified this change the task for the student of the period is to distinguish between those authors and dancers who adopted the adjective German to signify their commitment to Nazi ideology, those who used it out of expediency and those who adopted it to secure their safety against a hostile regime. For instance, it is most likely that Wigman's book of the period *Deutsche Tanzkunst* (1935) could be considered in the last category. The contrary position is well illustrated in Koegler's (1974) survey of articles from *Der Tanz*: he draws attention to Böhme's seminal article 'Is Ballet German?'

(1933) in which the author concludes that it cannot be because it is unsuited to the German national character.

The point to be taken from these examples is that there are times when substantial research outside the area of dance is necessary to give an accurate interpretation of source material within. The 1930s in Germany was an era when political events impinged directly on dance. This is less clearly the case in other countries and during other times. A general knowledge of the historical area under study should alert the student to features which are directly pertinent to dance history. Once alerted, the student should be able to notice apparent peculiarities and inconsistencies which require explanation in terms of the time and place in which they originated.

Selection of material

In looking at the early stages of any new form, in this case early European modern dance, it is first necessary to retrace the steps of its formation through accounts of known practitioners or significant events. These may well be secondary sources in the beginning leading to primary sources as they become available. It is only when the full extent of the dance of the period has been ascertained that the work of artists which has endured can be located and evaluated within the form as a whole. An excellent example of this process can be found in recent re-evaluations of the art of the Weimar period that had been ignored, lost, or forgotten since World War II (see, for example, Willett 1978).

Assuming that most of the relevant sources have been located, that these sources have been scrutinised and evaluated, the next major problem becomes that of defining the limits of the study and the criteria for the selection of material to be used. Needless to say the central concern should be dance, and criteria are dependent on the three central features established earlier – *choreography, performance* and *appreciation*. However, when considering modern dance as a form, and early European modern dance in particular, it is insufficient to assume the existence of a 'form' and to select material accordingly. Rather, the converse is true. The historical task is to seek those features in the dance and the work of dancers that allows a 'form' to be established. This task is easier at certain times than at others.

The following example considers just one aspect of selection: the direct relevance of certain dance activities to an understanding of

155

modern dance as a form. In most historical studies of twentieth-century dance theatre forms consideration is paid almost exclusively to professional dancers. However, in Germany, particularly during the 1920s, there were numerous dance groups made up of amateurs and students: these lay dancers, *Laientänzer*, often performed together in movement choirs, *Bewegungschöre*. Taken separately, the lay dancers' activities, massed dancing for the appreciation of the participants, differed markedly from those of the professionals in the theatre or on the concert stage. However, in a number of cases von Laban in particular choreographed on these lay dancers for public performances. Equally, both he and Wigman used the formal aspects of movement choir choreography in their theatre presentations. More significantly a number of von Laban's choreographies for his theatre company required the participation of large groups of dancers and these were recruited from the lay movement choirs. The implication is that aspects of the choreography and training of the dancers had features held in common by both types of practitioner despite the fact that the purpose of the dance and its appreciation differed markedly: in the case of the lay dancer the appreciation was primarily for the dancer rather than for an audience. With these features in mind it becomes necessary to include lay dancers in any study of dance of the 1910–33 period.

The significant question is whether such features of a dance form are contributory factors to the form as a whole or whether they are significant only in characterising a particular period. It is most important to be aware of, and to make explicit, the distinction.

8.3 *The study of modern dance as a distinctive form: approaches and topics*

This final section draws on the methodology described earlier to suggest various types of *approach* and *subject matter*. It has been indicated that, when studying a dance form, selection of material is of particular importance. In choosing a topic it is best to err on the side of a narrowly defined subject either in time or through time. The following examples, drawn mainly from European modern dance, illustrate the ways in which this approach may be employed without limiting the scope of a study.

In-depth study of a concise historical period in modern dance
Such a study may involve the selection of a period of interest that

arises from the extensive survey of the form in secondary sources.

e.g. *American and European modern dance in America following the arrival of Hanya Holm in New York: 1931–39.*

The delineation of geographical scope should also be precisely stated: whether in one country, two countries or internationally. As a general rule the geographical scope should be balanced by the length of the historical period in order that a coherent subject area is retained. A wide geographical area limits the historical area:

e.g. *Modern dance in Germany, Austria and America at the time of Martha Graham's emergence as a solo artist 1926–29.*

and conversely:

e.g. *Modern dance in Berlin during the period 1920–36 with reference to European artists and visiting American dancers.*

The emphasis in this type of study is on what went on. Periodicals and books provide a most useful source here, backed up where possible by company or dance school archives. A good example of the study of a concise, stated historical period is Koegler's review of 'dance in Germany 1927–1936' (1974). One consideration for this type of study is the difficulty of isolating the period in question. This involves deciding whether knowledge of what happened before and afterwards should be taken into account and if so how this can best be summarised.

Genealogical study of modern dance

There are many possibilities for the further study of family trees in modern dance as in other forms. Whilst there is some value in the drawing of a genealogical tree in itself, the main purpose of such a quest should be to use the structure to lead into a historical study through time. A basic structure of who worked with whom and when may be purely descriptive but the purpose should be to try to identify features of choreography and performance that have resulted from choreographer/dancer or teacher/pupil relationships.

e.g. *Hanya Holm as a teacher. Surviving features of European style in American modern dance.*

Dance school or company records and programmes may prove to be particularly fruitful sources with which to begin the detailing of such a study. Biographical accounts may indicate areas of influence that may be pursued. The writing of dance critics who are particularly aware of a dance form's lineage is similarly useful.

It should be recognised that the type of *influence* may differ according to the historical context. Three typical kinds of influence attributed to people are most commonly found. Firstly, as in early American modern dance, a straight genealogical development is readily discernible among those dancers who served a long and close apprenticeship with Graham, Humphrey or Holm. Secondly, there is the increasingly common case of a dancer working for short periods with numerous choreographers in various types of performance. Thirdly, there is the kind of influence that is often most difficult to establish where a dancer attributes 'influence' to a brief acquaintance. The last of these is particularly important for early European modern dance where many of von Laban's pupils opened schools in his name after a short apprenticeship and without his approval. These examples should illustrate why a family tree is only a starting point.

Longitudinal study to show changes within a dance form through time in choreography, performance and appreciation
In the historical study of dance forms, and of modern dance in particular, the form may change through time, internationally or culturally but the common features of choreography, performance and appreciation remain recognisable. They can be used to anchor facts and values in a seemingly wide-ranging topic. Although these three concepts cannot be regarded as independent of one another they can, either in themselves or in their sub-categories, act as a focus in the approaches illustrated below. Because these studies are followed through time, it is particularly important that the chosen concept is established in terms of the form as a whole and, when using examples, within the form at a particular time.

The following examples concentrate on topics that attempt to identify features of choreography, performance and appreciation of particular importance to the identification of modern dance as a recognisable form.

Choreography
　　e.g. *Choreography with percussion: a feature of modern dance 1910–80.*
Such a study would attempt to distinguish a feature of modern dance choreography: the use of percussion, which has at various periods been associated with modern dance. This would require not only identifying percussion as a device but also locating its use

historically: that is to say recognising those periods, particularly the 1920s and 1930s, where percussion was used by some choreographers almost exclusively. Not only did choreographers of this period use this type of music but its use was inextricably linked with their notions of what modern dance meant as a form, hence the artistic intentions of choreographers become important. In this instance their intentions were often made explicit in their writing (see, for instance, Wigman 1975).

Performance

e.g. *The Green Table in performance. Interpretations by Ballets Jooss and other companies from 1932 to the present.*

This example has been chosen to illustrate how performance itself is historically located. Such a subject should be considered initially in terms of how the work has been reconstructed for companies other than Ballets Jooss. This raises the topic of different interpretations given by ballet and modern dance companies (e.g. Joffrey Ballet and Batsheva Dance Company respectively). Such interpretations need to be located within the period in which they were performed: for instance, those performances given before the war that Jooss anticipated could be compared with those given after it.

Appreciation

Both choreography and performance require consideration of critical writing to illuminate them as topics. It is also possible to focus on appreciation itself using critical writing as a primary source.

e.g. *The role of the critic in forming a view of modern dance as a distinctive form.*

Particular critics could be identified in different countries at different periods: Brandenburg in pre-war Germany, Coton in England, Martin in pre-war America and more recently Croce, Jowitt and Banes. The task would be to identify the features of modern dance upon which the critic bases an evaluation, to locate these within the relevant period and to identify them within the changing nature of the form as a whole. Critical writing would, naturally, be a major source but it would also be necessary to refer such writing back to the dance performance itself wherever possible and also using recorded material if it is available.

159

The study of dancers and choreographers in modern dance
Much of dance history consists of straightforward accounts of the work of individual dancers as performers and/or choreographers. When the emphasis is on the study of a dance form, there is no reason why a representative dancer cannot be chosen to act as a focus. However, it would be wrong to think that merely describing the work of one of the better-known dancers of a period necessarily gives insight into the form. (The problematic nature of the role of the individual as artist in art history is ably examined in Wolff 1981). It is preferable, when considering the work of individual dancers, to place them within a topic that acknowledges the concepts of period, choreography, performance and appreciation, hence:

> e.g. *Women's dance groups in modern dance with particular reference to Mary Wigman's group 1920–26.*

Conclusion

This chapter has examined some aspects of modern dance as a form. In looking at early European modern dance in particular, certain considerations have been highlighted. Naming and consensus views have been shown to cause difficulties if taken at face value and the need to identify distinctive concepts has been stressed. Problems of translation highlight the difficulties of using source material. More importantly, they emphasise the need to locate a dance form both historically and culturally. These considerations should be approached as challenges rather than stumbling blocks and the topic examples given show the diversity of approach suggested by early European modern dance as a subject and the value of structuring dance history in terms of choreography, performance and appreciation.

References
Böhme, F. 1933 'Ist Ballett Deutsch?' *Deutsche Allgemeine Zeitung* (25 April)
Brandenburg, H. 1921 *Der moderne Tanz* (2nd ed.). Munich: G. Müller
Brown, J. M. (ed.) 1980 *The vision of modern dance*. London: Dance Books

Cohen, S. J. (ed.) 1977 *Dance as a theatre art: source readings in dance history from 1581 to the present*. London: Dance Books

Hall, F. 1950 *Modern English ballet: an interpretation*. London: Melrose

Hamby, C. 1978 'Dance in education – is it an adventure into the world of art? Part 1', *Laban Art of Movement Guild Magazine*, 60 (May) pp. 11–29

Knust, A. 1979 *Dictionary of Kinetography Laban (Labanotation)*, vols. 1 & 2. London: Macdonald & Evans

Koegler, H. 1972 'Tanz in die Dreissiger Jahre', *Ballett 1972*. Velber: Friedrich

Koegler, H. 1974 'In the shadow of the swastika: dance in Germany, 1927–1936', *Dance Perspectives*, 57 (Spring)

Laban, R. von 1930 *Script dancing – La danse écrite*. Vienna: Universal Edition

Laban, R. von 1935 *Ein Leben für den Tanz. Erinnerungen*. Dresden: C. Reissner

Laban, R. 1975 *A life for dance: reminiscences* (trans from 1935 ed. and annot. by L. Ullmann). London: Macdonald & Evans

Martin, J. 1933, 1965 *The modern dance*. Republ. New York: Dance Horizons

Maynard, O. 1965 *American modern dancers: the pioneers*. Boston: Little, Brown

McDonagh, D. 1976 *The complete guide to modern dance*. New York: Doubleday

Murray, J. 1979 *Dance now*. Harmondsworth: Penguin

Patterson, M. 1981 *The revolution in German theatre 1900–1933*. London: Routledge & Kegan Paul

Wigman, M. 1933, 1977 'The philosophy of modern dance', *Europa* 1. No. 1 (May–July), repr. in Cohen, S. J.

Wigman, M. 1935 *Deutsche Tanzkunst*. Dresden: C. Reissner.

Wigman, M. 1975 *The Mary Wigman book* (ed. and trans. by W. Sorell). Middletown, Conn.: Wesleyan University Press

Willett, J. 1978 *The new sobriety 1917–1933: art and politics in the Weimar period*. London: Thames & Hudson

Wolff, J. 1981 *The social production of art*. London: Macmillan

CHAPTER 9

Traditional dance: English ceremonial and social forms

by Theresa Buckland

9.1 Previous scholarship
9.2 Written source materials
9.3 Selection of an area of study

Traditional or 'folk' dances as they are often known can be distinguished from other forms of dance by the fact that they are
handed down from generation to generation *without close reference to
national or international standards*.

Traditional dances may begin their existence in the fashionable
ballroom or, indeed, in the theatre. In many cases their origin
cannot be discovered. However, the task of the student of the history
of traditional dance is not to concentrate solely on origins but to
extend present knowledge of the nature of the form, its context and
transmission in the past.

The traditional dances of England can be broadly classified into
two major groups; those dances which are executed at particular
times of the year in a performer/audience context, and those which
are not tied to the calendar and are performed mainly for
recreational purposes. The former group are referred to here as
ceremonial dances and the latter as *social dances*.

Ceremonial dancing in England is traditionally most frequently
performed by men, although there are notable exceptions, especially
in the north-west region. Morris and Sword Dancing (see Cawte
et al. 1960) constitute the two most common forms of English
ceremonial dancing. Social dancing in England usually involves
simultaneous participation by both sexes. The majority of these
types of dances, however, have their origin in the fashionable
ballroom or, if derived from other sources, at least existed in this

context at some time. The characteristics of the two groups described above are not totally distinct as there are several dances which at any one time may display both ceremonial and social features.

9.1 *Previous scholarship*

Perhaps the most famous date in the history of English traditional dance scholarship is Boxing Day 1899. It was on this day that Cecil Sharp first witnessed the performance of a Morris team.

Although he noted down the tunes which accompanied the dances, Sharp did not attempt to collect the choreography until 1905. In this year Mary Neal, who organised an association for underprivileged girls in East London known as the 'Esperance Working Girls' Club', approached Sharp with a request for traditional English dances for the girls to perform. Thus began the attempt to collect folk dances before, as was feared, urbanisation and industrialisation destroyed the rural setting where the traditional dance culture appeared to flourish.

Many dances were undoubtedly either in a dead or moribund state and it cannot be disputed that, had Sharp and his fellow collectors delayed in their task, our knowledge of traditional dancing in the second half of the nineteenth century would be infinitely poorer. In 1911 Sharp founded the English Folk Dance Society with the purpose of fostering the revival of English traditional dance. The collections of traditional dances published by Sharp and his associates form the main corpus of material employed in the revival and set out the 'pagan origin' theory of traditional dance which has remained unchallenged until this decade in English publications.

In his theoretical writing on traditional dance Sharp concentrated on origins. This orientation he shared with nineteenth century folklorists from whom, albeit indirectly at first, he drew his interpretation of folk custom.

The theory of cultural survival, formulated by the anthropologist E. B. Tyler and popularised by Sir James Frazer (1890) in *The Golden Bough*, stated that all traditional customs had their origin in primitive rituals which still lingered in the countryside. Although there was no sound historical evidence to support this theory, it gained wide credence and remains today in many writings on traditional dance.

163

The effect of this theory was to channel the collecting activities of those interested in traditional dance into searching the countryside for any vestiges of a primitive dance culture. The towns and cities were ignored. Consequently, traditional dance types such as the Morris dancing of the north-west and the widespread traditions of solo step-dancing often found in urban areas were not systematically collected.

An examination of the notes of early collectors such as Sharp, Maud Karpeles and Clive Carey reveal what today would be regarded as unmethodical collection, lack of social and historical data, and a restricting belief that the purest form of traditional dance never alters its choreography except for the worse.

This latter point is again a feature of nineteenth century folklorist theory: change and variation are thought to be indicative of degeneration from the primitive and pure archetype. Such an attitude demonstrates a misunderstanding of the nature of traditional dance.

However, with no historical records of the choreography available to the collectors, it was impossible for them to gain a historical perspective based on factual evidence. Furthermore social class differences between collector and informant supported the misleading notion of the uneducated, unreflective tradition-bearer who had little of real significance to offer other than the dance itself. Instead of concentrating upon the obtainable facts from informants, the collector preferred to speculate upon the origins of the dance in inaccessible antiquity.

9.2 *Written source materials*

There is in fact no general written introduction to English traditional dance to be recommended which does not suffer from inaccuracies or speculations. A recent publication, Hugh Rippon's (1975) *Discovering English Folk Dance*, is perhaps the best and most concise introduction to date and is particularly illuminating on the interplay between the tradition and the revival.

The standard manuals on the performance of traditional dance are those produced in the early decades of this century chiefly by Sharp. *A Handbook of Morris Dances* by Lionel Bacon (1974) is a more comprehensive 'aide-memoire' with regard to ceremonial dance and the *Community Dance Manuals* published by the English Folk Dance and Song Society (E.F.D.S.S.) between 1947 and 1967, have made available in written form a larger repertoire of social dances.

More specialised articles can be found mainly in the *Folk Music Journal*, formerly known as the *Journal of the English Folk Dance and Song Society*. Bibliographic sheets of the dance articles from the journal's inception are available from the Vaughan Williams Memorial Library at the headquarters, Cecil Sharp House, London. The magazine *English Dance and Song*, which is now published three times a year, contains relevant material and is also held in the Vaughan Williams Memorial Library. There is a published catalogue of the library's holding which is the largest collection of information on English traditional dance including archival film, photographs and sound recordings, in addition to manuscript and published material.

Other organisations in England which produce periodicals on traditional dance are the Morris Ring, an association of men's ceremonial dance teams founded by revival groups in 1934, and the Women's Morris Federation, the female equivalent, established in 1975. The Morris Ring publish *The Morris Dancer* three times a year, which is chiefly concerned with ceremonial dance and includes articles both on the traditional form and its revival. *Morris Matters* published on a quarterly basis by Windsor Morris in association with the Women's Morris Federation tends to be more popular and controversial, although some authors contribute to both *Morris Matters* and *The Morris Dancer*.

The Morris Ring has begun a policy of organising and expanding its archives and any bona fide researcher may consult its collection of photographs, film and written material. It holds addresses of practically all existing male ceremonial dance teams and publishes, in addition to its own catalogue of archival photographs, lists of ceremonial dance articles in the *Folk Music Journal* and *English Dance and Song*.

The Women's Morris Federation is also intent on following a similar policy and, in addition on making dance notations available. However, the sources for these notations should be checked carefully before accepting them as an authentic record of a traditional performance. This is because some notations may derive from a freely interpreted reconstruction by a revival group.

Unfortunately a preliminary checklist of traditional social dances in England does not exist and reference has to be made to the footnotes and bibliographies, where given, in various publications. Researchers of ceremonial dance have a better resource in the indices of the geographical distribution of these dances compiled respectively by Needham (1936) and Cawte *et al.* (1960). The 1936 index lists all located references known at that time to ceremonial dance since 1800. The 1960 index extends its historical references to all known located records. There are inaccuracies and some omissions from this index (now in need of revision) but it does identify the chief characteristics of the regional forms and provides a ready checklist of sources.

9.3 *Selection of an area of study*

There has been little detailed work on the history of traditional dancing in England and there exists a wide field for investigation. The student may select a particular geographical area, for example, and discover the various types of traditional dancing once practised there. Alternatively, one type of traditional dance could be chosen and the various contexts in which this type appeared investigated.

The study of the history of traditional dancing can be divided into:

9.3.1 Dances beyond living memory

9.3.2 Dances within living memory

Sources for the first group are to be found mainly in written form, whereas the second group may consist of both written and oral sources.

There remain relatively few folk dancers today who can demonstrate a tradition which has been passed on to them orally and kinetically from the nineteenth century. Such rare individuals have already become the focus of study by those interested in traditional dancing.

Some students may know of traditional dance forms through either their own active involvement or possibly through that of their family and friends. Such first-hand knowledge of an area presents an ideal starting point for study.

Clearly new traditions have arisen since the last century, particularly within the revival movement. These traditions of perhaps only two or three generations present exciting new material to study. Since the early years of this century, new ceremonial dance teams have sprung up all over the country, and numerous events take place at which revived traditional social dance can be seen. These new developments need to be studied through both written and oral sources in addition to witnessing actual performances.

Revivals prior to those begun by the English Folk Dance and Song Society also require investigation. For example, the church and/or school within a community may have acted as patrons or even instigators of dancing. Very often introductions of ceremonial events such as May Day festivals were made which contained dance performances. Sometimes these introductions transformed already existing local customs into occasions for children who took on the main participants' roles instead of adults.

It is clear that any attempt to account for the form of traditional dance must take the social and historical context into account.

9.3.1 *Dances beyond living memory*

The primary sources which make reference to traditional dance are classified in chronological order below, although some types of material may occur in more than one historical period. Since the student is likely to be dealing with local history material, the reference works by Stephens (1973) and Richardson (1974) will be invaluable in understanding the techniques used.

Churchwardens' accounts

These records are generally kept at the parish churches or the local and diocesan record offices. They can be particularly valuable for details of costume and properties used in traditional ceremonial dances and for information on the payment of the performers, e.g.

1521–22 Eight yerds of fustyan for the Mores-daunsars coats 0.16.0

(Kingston-upon-Thames Churchwardens'

Accounts, quoted in Burton (1891) p.106).

The church was responsible in varying degrees for the organisation of celebrations of holy days. Some of the dancing activities watched over by the church were utilised to raise money for charitable purposes as at Abbots Bromley, Staffordshire.

Dance manuals

These exist in both manuscript and published form and are held chiefly in public and university libraries. The student should in particular consult the collections at Cecil Sharp House. Much of the published material does not deal with contemporary traditional dance but with popular and fashionable forms which may later become part of the traditional repertoire. There are no known British manuals of ceremonial dance predating the twentieth century revival.

Diaries, journals, topographies, gazeteers

Many personal diaries such as that by Nicholas Blundell (1712), which contains a reference to an eighteenth century performance of a Sword Dance near Liverpool, have been published. However, it is likely that many diaries and journals are held in local libraries which have not yet been consulted for references to traditional forms of dance. Most early diaries were written by people with leisure and education and thus tend to reflect upper or middle class attitudes towards traditional dancing. Therefore knowledge of the social status of the writer is vital to the interpretation of the record. Upper class society is not always necessarily adverse to traditional customs, nor are men of more humble origins equally well disposed.

A type of publication which sometimes contains references to traditional dancing is the topography, a description of an area's natural and artificial features. Topographies were popular from the seventeenth to the early nineteenth centuries, and since they were often written on a county basis are most useful for discovering references to local instances of ceremonial dancing. Thus Robert Plot's *Natural History of Staffordshire* of 1686 (p. 434) contains the earliest known description of the Abbots Bromley Horn Dance. Similarly, gazeteers may also include details of dance customs performed at particular feast or market days in the year although they are generally not the best sources for references to social forms of traditional dancing.

Newspapers and periodicals

From the second half of the nineteenth century (and earlier in cities and some large towns) the student's task is enormously eased by the growth in local newspapers. Most local libraries hold back copies, or issues can be consulted at the newspaper section of the British Library.

Reports of ceremonial dance are again easier to locate than those of social dance. With the former's appearance at certain times of the year the potential field is clearly narrowed. However, it is necessary to be alert to changing patterns of ceremonial behaviour in the locality. For example, Morris dances were performed at the traditional time of the local wakes in north-west England, sometime between June and September. But reports of these occurrences became increasingly rare at the turn of the century and searches through the newspaper are more rewarding thereafter if references to May festivals, rose queen fêtes and carnivals held in the spring and summer months are found. Advance notices of ceremonial dancing were by no means uncommon in the local press of that area. In addition to advertisements there are occasional accounts of Morris dancers practising in the streets before the commencement of the wakes holiday. Sometimes newspaper references to Morris dancers after their performance date can be found when their names and activities are recorded in the list of court appearances together with charges of drunkenness or trespassing.

Accounts of social dancing in traditional contexts tend to be rare except in brief references to competitive step dancing in the advertisements placed by publicans to attract patrons to their houses during festive periods. It is also possible to find the occasional article of reminiscences about past local life which may include a description of the local social dance gatherings.

As with all dance material, the student must investigate the political, proprietary and religious sympathies, in this case, of the newspaper. In the early 1860s, the Oldham press was extremely sympathetic towards local customs whereas in the very same period, the Rochdale papers, anxious to advertise the town as being at the forefront of Victorian progress and rationalism, supported the campaign against traditional celebrations. In Oldham Morris dancing continued to flourish at the end of the nineteenth century, but it appears to have died out during this period in Rochdale.

Folklore and local history collections
In the second half of the nineteenth century, references to ceremonial dancing increased with the development of local history and folklore studies. Where these contain eyewitness accounts of traditional dancing such sources can be classified as primary. A related source is the biography which may include information on traditional dancing either witnessed or practised in the author's youth.

Historical novels
Historical novels often contain references to traditional dances but

these cannot be regarded as primary sources for the particular period in which the novel is placed unless the author is recalling a personal experience and setting it in the appropriate time span. Examples of novelists who use this device are Thomas Hardy (1872), referred to in this respect in Chapter 2, and the Lancashire author Ben Brierley (1884 a, b) who described Morris dancing at the wakes. Nevertheless, such sources need to be checked against contemporary accounts since the novelist is not necessarily concerned to present a faithful record of remembered events.

Folk dance collections

The majority of collections of English traditional dance are housed at the Vaughan Williams Memorial Library. Locations of other manuscripts containing references to ceremonial dances are given in Cawte *et al.* (1960).

However, much material still remains in the hands of the original collectors and is not as yet readily available.

Costume, regalia, photographs, film

Occasionally actual dance items such as dancing clogs are donated to museums. Unfortunately, the Cecil Sharp House collection of various artefacts of English traditional dancing was bomb-damaged.

With the developing interest in the daily life of the past, many libraries are beginning to build up collections of old photographs depicting local life. These may include photographs of ceremonial dance teams. The Manchester Studies department of Manchester Polytechnic possesses two interesting films of morris dancers at Whalley, Lancashire, in 1913 and 1919. Such rare visual records provide numerous starting points for study including, in this case, the possibility of analysing changes over a short period of time.

9.3.2 Dances within living memory

All the listings in the above section are also potential source material for the study of traditional dances within living memory. However, in the study of dances within living memory additional valuable information may be obtained from former participants.

Memories of former performers are best recorded on tape to ensure accuracy and to communicate something of the character of the informant. Quotations from dancers help to illuminate the material from the human angle. Not only should students who are about to engage in collecting information from people familiarise themselves completely with operating their tape recorders, but they should also practise interviewing techniques before starting fieldwork in order to achieve the maximum of freely given information from their interviewees with the minimum number of questions. Of particular help in preparing to conduct interviews are Goldstein's (1964) publication and that of Ives (1980).

The performers

In the past very little emphasis was placed on the individuals who were involved in traditional dancing. Modern folklore study, however, recognises that details such as the participants' age, sex, occupation and social status need to be collected in order to gain some understanding of the nature of traditional dancing.

Dancing styles are often transmitted through families, particularly in solo forms such as step-dancing, although in the South Midlands kinship also played a vital role in the composition of Morris teams. Sometimes dance styles are the property of particular occupations such as the modified form of Lancashire step-dancing performed by the lifeboatmen of Cromer, Norfolk. Investigations need to be made into the composition of *revival* dance teams in this respect.

It is important to ascertain how and why dancers become involved in their chosen style and also to discover how much or how little they had been exposed to it before participating. Dancers within revival groups may have joined after witnessing a public performance of a local team or through participation in some other aspect of the folk revival movement, such as being a member of a folk song club.

Distinctive modes of learning and rehearsing also need to be closely investigated. In Bampton, one traditional Morris team meets only a few weeks before their traditional day of Spring Bank Holiday Monday to practise, whereas at Bacup the coconut dancers aim to rehearse once a week throughout the year. Practice nights are often social occasions as well as periods set aside to learn or maintain the performance of particular movements.

Occasions of performance

Most of the literature tends to refer to the traditional times of performance during the year and consequently our assessment of dancers' responses to changing social contexts is inadequate. Much information on the times of performance with regard to ceremonial dance can be gleaned from written records, particularly newspapers, and from former participants.

Informants should be questioned about all types of performance and about the existence and type of other activities taking place on the same occasion. Seemingly contradictory information on the routes undertaken by teams may be explained by changes introduced from year to year on the grounds of available time, personal choice and economics. The collection of money and hospitality shown by patrons to the dancers in the form of food and drink have a particular effect upon the choice of route. Ceremonial dancers in the past needed at least to cover their own expenditure and preferably earn some money from their exertions.

The dance

The chief rules in the collection of dance notations are to let the former participant provide the terminology and to avoid any demonstration of steps oneself since this might itself distort and bias the response.

In the case of revival teams detailed enquiries should be made with regard to the source of the dance notation. If this is a written source, it should be checked carefully against the notations offered by former dancers and, where relevant, against the dance as it is presently performed. Variations may have occurred over the years and it is important to note them. It is also useful to realise that individual variations within a group dance may, in some instances, have been desirable. This may account for apparent discrepancies between notations collected from different dancers. Such apparent discrepancies may also derive from differences in choreography and performance over time.

The whole repertoire of dances should always be collected.

The music

Dancers and musicians have different perceptions of the performance and, accordingly, should be interviewed both separately and jointly if possible. This is especially valuable in determining timing and phrasing. All musicians with any connection with the dancers should be recorded both playing and reminiscing. The provenance of the music, how the musician came to be involved in the tradition, the process of learning the music, and her/his attitude towards it should all be investigated.

172

Costume and regalia

Queries regarding the dress for traditional dancing are as relevant to studies of social dancing as they are to considerations of the more obviously special attire of ceremonial dancers. Types of dress alter to suit the occasion, and footwear, in particular, has a marked effect upon the dance style.

Many of England's ceremonial dancers use properties such as sticks, swords and handkerchiefs, and the acquisition of those must be investigated. Information should also be acquired on the properties of the supernumeraries, such as hobbyhorses, fools and man/woman figures, which sometimes accompany traditional ceremonial dance teams.

Conclusion

Even if the student wishes to concentrate on one aspect of traditional dancing, e.g. the costume or the occasions of performance, the other components of the dance event must not be ignored. Characteristic relationships between particular types of dance and the environment, between costume and local industries, between the choice of musical instruments and the form of the dance, etc., may have existed and require discussion.

As folk dance studies in England exist at present, there are few detailed historical studies available. There does exist, however, a wide range of primary sources, both written and oral, which, when investigated, will not only deepen and broaden understanding of the form, transmission and context of traditional dancing in the past, but will also considerably illuminate the role of dance in society today. Of particular importance in this respect is the need for the studies of traditional dance to be carried out on a local basis.

References

Bacon, L. 1974 *A handbook of Morris dances*. The Morris Ring

Blundell, N. 1712 *The great diurnal of Nicholas Blundell of Little Crosby, Lancashire*, vol. 2, 1712–19, ed. by J. J. Bagley 1970. The Record Society of Lancashire and Cheshire. See entries for July 3, 7, 8, 9, pp. 25–26

Brierley, B. 1884a 'Trevor Hall' *Tales and sketches of Lancashire life. The chronicles of Waverlow*. Manchester: Abel Heywood & Son; London: Simpkin Marshall & Co. See esp. pp. 126–32

Brierley, B. 1884b 'Christmas at Ringwood Hal!', *Tales and sketches of Lancashire life. Marlocks of Merriton. Red Windows Hall.* Manchester: Abel Heywood & Son; London: Simpkin, Marshall. See esp. pp. 148–9

Buckland, T. (ed.) 1982 *Traditional dance,* vol. 1. Proceedings of the Traditional Dance Conference held at Crewe and Alsager College of Higher Education, 1981. Alsager: Crewe & Alsager College of Higher Education

Buckland, T. (ed.) 1983 *Traditional dance: historical perspectives,* vol. 2. Alsager: Crewe & Alsager College of Higher Education

Burton, A. 1891 *Rush bearing.* Manchester: Brook & Chrystal

Cawte, E. C., Helm, A., Marriott, R. J., Peacock, N. 1961 'A Geographical Index of the Ceremonial Dance in Great Britain', *Journal of the English Folk Dance and Song Society,* vol. IX, no. 1, pp. 1–41

Cawte, E. C., Helm, A., Marriott, R. J., Peacock, N. 1961 'Addenda and Corrigenda', *J.E.F.D.S.S.,* vol. IX, no. 2 (1961), pp. 93–95

English Folk Dance and Song Society 1947–67 *The community dance manuals* vols. 1–7. London: English Folk Dance and Song Society

Frazer, J. G. 1890, 1900 *The Golden Bough, a study in comparative religion,* (2 vols.), 2nd ed. 3 vols. London: Macmillan

Frazer, J. G. 1907–15 *The Golden Bough, a study in magic and religion.* 3rd ed. 12 vols. (paperback 1957, rep. 1976) London: Macmillan

Goldstein, K. S. 1964 *A guide for field workers in folklore.* Hatboro, Pennsylvania: Folklore Associates; London: Herbert Jenkins

Hardy, T. 1872, 1974 *Under the Greenwood Tree or The Mellstock Quire. A rural painting of the Dutch school.* London: Macmillan. See esp. pp. 52–59

Ives, E. D. 1980 *The tape-recorded interview: a manual for field workers in folklore and oral history.* Knoxville, U.S.A.: University of Tennessee Press

Needham, J. 1936 'The Geographical Distribution of the English Ceremonial Dance Traditions', *J.E.F.D.S.S.,* vol. III, no. 1., pp. 1–45

Plot, R. 1686, 1973 *The natural history of Staffordshire.* Oxford: printed at the Theater, p. 434 facs; Didsbury: E. J. Morten

Richardson, J. 1974, 1975, 1977 *The local historian's encyclopedia.* New Barnet, Herts: Historical Publications

Rippon, H. 1975, 1981 *Discovering English folk dance.* Aylesbury, Bucks.: Shire Publications

Sharp, C. J. 1907–14 *The Morris book.* London: Novello (5 parts)
Part 1 with MacIlwaine, H. C. (1st ed. 1907, 2nd ed. 1912); (rep. 1974) Wakefield: E.P. Publishing
Part 2 with MacIlwaine, H. C. (1st ed. 1909, 2nd ed. 1919); (rep. 1974) Wakefield: E.P. Publishing
Part 3 with MacIlwaine, H. C. (1st ed. 1910, 2nd ed. 1924); (rep. 1974) Wakefield: E.P. Publishing
Part 4 (1st ed. 1911); (rep. 1975) Wakefield: E.P. Publishing
Part 5 with Butterworth, G. (1st ed. 1913); (rep. 1975) Wakefield: E.P. Publishing
Sharp, C. J. 1909–22 *The country dance books* (6 parts)
Part 1 (1st ed. 1909, 2nd ed. 1934) rev. & ed. Karpeles, M.; (rep. 1972) Wakefield: E.P. Publishing
Part 2 (1st ed. 1911, 2nd ed. 1913, 3rd ed. 1927); (rep. 1972) Wakefield: E.P. Publishing
Part 3 with Butterworth, G. (1st ed. 1912, 2nd ed. 1927); (rep. 1975) Wakefield: E.P. Publishing
Part 4 with Butterworth, G. (1st ed. 1916, 2nd ed. 1918, 3rd ed. 1927); (rep. 1975) Wakefield: E.P. Publishing
Part 5 with Karpeles, M. (1st ed. 1918); (rep. 1976) Wakefield: E. P. Publishing
Part 6 (1st ed. 1922, 2nd ed. 1927); (rep. 1976) Wakefield: E.P. Publishing
Sharp, C. J. 1911–13 *The Sword dances of Northern England* (3 parts)
Part 1 (1st ed. 1911, 2nd ed. 1950) ed. Karpeles, M.; (rep. 1977) Wakefield: E.P. Publishing
Part 2, (1st ed. 1913, 2nd ed. 1951) ed. Karpeles, M.; (rep. 1977) Wakefield: E.P. Publishing
Part 3 (1st ed. 1913, 2nd ed. 1951) ed. Karpeles, M.; (rep. 1977) Wakefield: E.P. Publishing
Stephens, W. B. 1973, 1975 *Sources for English local history.* Manchester: University Press. U.S.A.: Rowman and Littlefield

PART IV

Guidelines for teaching and learning dance history

The emphasis in Part IV is the educational application of the approaches presented in Parts II and III. We consider how a curriculum unit in dance history might be constructed and on the kind of work a student might undertake in consequence of following a dance history course.

In Chapter 10 principles of curriculum design are related to the specific content of dance as art, in the Western world, in the twentieth century. A 'unit', or area of study, is mapped out with a description of a number of possible routes within it. In principle the area of study could be used with any age group although the depth and complexity of the work would, of course, be different.

Students following such courses would normally be expected to write an essay or dissertation or to produce some piece of work as evidence of understanding. This frequently takes the form of an investigation by an individual into a specific topic of interest. Guidelines for structuring a historical investigation, both in terms of processes that might be used and of writing up the work, are the subject of Chapter 11.

CHAPTER 10

Constructing curriculum units in dance history

by Janet Adshead and Joan W. White

10.1 Making a curriculum unit
10.2 A foundation unit in dance history
10.3 Possible routes for study

In contrast with previous sections of this text attention here is specifically on the educational implications and, therefore, on the application of the rationale, methodology and content of dance history to the dance curriculum. Some possibilities in the use of different kinds of dance sources were outlined in Part II, and for the study of diverse forms of dance in Part III. An attempt is made in this chapter to find a way of using these structures to formulate a valid and interesting course of study for beginners in dance history. The intention is that this unit, or parts of it, could be studied by students of different ages. For example, eleven-year-old pupils, C.S.E. or G.C.E. groups, undergraduate or postgraduate students could all, in their own quite distinct ways, make use of this material. The breadth and/or depth of investigation might vary – for example, the complex relationships which exist between different aspects of the content might form a substantial part of an advanced study while a simple chronological or genealogical account would suffice for eleven year olds. In other words, the content remains constant, as a bank of knowledge, while its use in a specific teaching situation is variable. Teaching situations vary because of differences in the teacher's aim; in the students' age; in experience of dance and its history; in the study methods with which students are familiar; in their capacity for written work and for independent study and so on.

The title of the proposed unit is 'A historical and cultural perspective of twentieth century Western theatre dance'. The selection of twentieth century theatre dance in the Western world was made on two main grounds:

a) Classical ballet and modern dance are major examples of *living* dance at the present moment. As such they are available for viewing and are more likely to catch the imagination of students than dance forms they cannot actually see.

b) Classical ballet and modern dance are also the major *forms* of dance taught in both state maintained and private institutions. This focus on the history of classical ballet and modern dance would, therefore, inform and relate to the rest of the dance study, whether it concerns dance composition, technique or criticism and whether it is of a practical or theoretical nature.

To start a history course with live dance forms is probably a sound choice in terms of motivation. Although classical ballet and modern dance can be demonstrated respectively to have their origins with Louis XIV and Isadora Duncan and her contemporaries, these personalities may appear somewhat remote today. They lack the immediate appeal that a practising ballet or modern dance choreographer or dancer has particularly for younger pupils. In time, and as the understanding of historical dance deepens, one would expect interest to develop and skills to be acquired for investigations into more distant periods of time. It is, however, just as possible to devise a unit based on traditional dance (or any other form) and possibly more relevant to do so in those parts of the country where other dance forms flourish and where little formal theatre is available.

The approach to study in this unit is twofold. On the one hand, the focus is on the structure of the dance itself and its development through time, and on the other hand, it is on the social and historical conditions of groups of artists. A number of artists can be seen to share certain characteristics and, grouped together, they might constitute a distinctive 'school' of dance.

This unit is an example of a chronological approach to dance history in which limited periods in time are identified. The time limits are not random but are determined by the occurrence, and indeed predominance, of certain forms and schools of dance. Only those which exist as art in a theatrical context, i.e. ballet and modern dance, are included.

179

10.1 *Making a curriculum unit*

In preparing a unit of study certain curriculum processes, which are well-established in educational practice, may provide a guide or a check list to ensure that relevant factors have been considered in setting out what one proposes to teach, how one proposes to teach it, and by what means one assesses the success of the enterprise.

The overall strategy of creating a 'unit' is concerned with devising a coherent, logical plan which will show a progression throughout but be self-contained. Boundaries are set in order that manageable 'chunks' can be isolated and taught. Distinctions have to be clear between the content (what is taught) and teaching methods (how it is taught). The way in which the course is evaluated or assessed is also a matter of great importance but one which makes sense only in relation to what the teacher sets out to do. In other words, the aims or intentions of the teacher are crucial in determining each stage of the curriculum process. As an example, if the aim is for students to understand how Martha Graham's style and dramatic intensity developed throughout her career, it would be inappropriate to assess the students' own ability to perform a contraction or to create their own dances. It might, however, be of value to perform short extracts from several of her dances spread over a time span, for the insights that this would offer.

The aims of the course indicate to the teacher how to proceed with the next stage of planning. In the Graham example this would involve studying the historical period in which her choreography first emerged as distinctively her own style. Perhaps by starting with the production of *Lamentation* in 1930 and tracing her dramatic dances through to *Clytemnestra* in 1958 students would be able to describe and analyse what it is that is so powerful about her use of movement.

The traditional curriculum model, then, is one of specifying aims, objectives, content, teaching methods and assessment procedures. There is no other clear model which asks the same sort of questions and, although some people would argue that it enforces too strict a pattern on the construction of courses and does not allow for flexibility to change direction in the actual teaching situation, what it does provide is an outline in the planning stage.

The unit is presented here in the normal format and then in diagrammatic form. The total, as it stands, would probably be suitable for a longer course than most dance teachers or lecturers have available for dance history, so it is subsequently divided up into a variety of routes to illustrate the possibilities for using smaller parts. Reasons are given for selecting some sections in combination with others.

The aim

The reasons for the title and overall selection of content have been given earlier in the chapter. The aim, a very general statement of intention, is deduced from that initial decision and merely states that students should acquire an understanding of 'a historical and cultural perspective of dance'. The emphasis is on *understanding* although this need not necessarily be only of a theoretical kind. It is often most appropriate to pursue historical study of the type described here through watching, discussing and writing about dance, resulting in either a verbal account or a written piece of work. It is possible, however, in principle and with competent dancers, to approach such study through learning how to perform parts of a particular dance in the appropriate style. It would take much longer and normal analytic methods would still have to be employed in order to ascertain whether the students had understood the historical developments of the dance. The average pupil or student is unlikely to have the physical skills to perform the dances mentioned here, although at degree level there is a possibility that extracts from some of the dances could be taught or demonstrated in order to point to change in style, in structure, and in performances of the works through time.

Objectives

The objectives of a course are derived from the aims and provide a more specific statement of intention. The generality of most aims would not allow detailed content to be described, hence the necessity of a statement of objectives. They divide the aim into several related, but separable, intentions. Thus the general aim of understanding the historical and cultural context of twentieth century Western theatre dance may be divided into two mutually supportive strands of enquiry, one concerning the development through time of *dances* in both the classical and modern forms and the second, the *cultural forces* which gave rise to similarities, to trends, to overall features which many choreographers of a particular era share in common. Thus the notion of an American, European or British school of dance might be seen to make sense. Each nation, country and continent has a complex identity in consequence of the social, political and artistic events which mould it through time. It would be surprising if European dance was not distinct from American dance given their different development as cultures in their own right.

Although the focus in teaching might be on one or other of these objectives, they are both important for a historical appreciation of dance since one gives access to the changing *dance* structure, the internal features, and the other to *reasons for change*, where they lie in the cultural context of a given period. Different dance styles are often the result of direct or indirect cultural influences.

Content

The content of the unit arises as a direct consequence of the statement of objectives. In relation to the first objective, *the study of the development of dances through time*, it is necessary to select specific dances to study. The selection made in the unit covers the relevant historical period, i.e. the twentieth century, and pinpoints significant events in the development of both classical ballet and modern dance. The detailed diagram presented on pp. 190–1, gives actual examples, while this first course outline only gives the periods and companies or choreographers to be studied, e.g. the Diaghilev Ballet in London 1911–29. The choice of individual dances may be made on the purely practical grounds of the availability of resources for study. All the dances listed in the unit are either still in the repertoire of the original (and/or other) companies or are readily available in other ways, e.g. on film.

The periods selected are not amenable to quite the same flexibility and choice as the dances. It could be argued that in order to have an understanding of the development of dance in this century one must know something of certain eras and individuals, e.g. of Diaghilev, Graham, etc.

The content described in the course outline gives an indication of the areas that might be covered in a series of lessons or lectures, although detailed plans are not provided. It is sufficient here merely to pinpoint what would seem to be some of the most important areas to study. Some overlap is unavoidable since developments in any one dance genre (form) do not necessarily cease because another emerges. In addition, there are parallel strands across the two major genres. One might focus on the *choreography*, i.e. on the detail of structural features or dynamic or spatial elements of selected dances and on the differences and similarities that are evident in the changing productions. Attention might be given to *performance* requirements, to the range of technical skills required, to the exact nature of the movements and to how these might have altered with changes in technique. Analysis of different *interpretations* of the same dance, e.g. de Valois' *Checkmate* performed in 1937 and 1980, would reveal features which remain constant and some which have changed. Emphasis might be placed on the views of critics, on writings about these particular dances and on how they have been *appraised* through time.

The staging, accompaniment and lighting are all important features of dance in a theatrical context and this is an area which could be examined profitably. At a more general level, analysis of the 'themes' or 'meanings' of dances from different periods would tell the student something of the social and artistic concerns which predominated in a particular era. This would relate closely to the second objective in requiring also an understanding of cultural developments.

The second objective, *the study of the cultural forces which relate to the dance*, requires a different approach. In the early chapters of this book a number of different starting points and types of historical study are identified. The second objective is an example where the total cultural context, embodied in general trends in artistic, social and political life, comes to the forefront. These trends relate to the dance in a number of ways, they may give rise to specific dances or find their first expression in dance and influence other arts. It is the relationship between these forces and the emerging dance forms that is of interest, if the dance is to remain at the centre of the study. The contrast with the first objective is that the concern is now in terms of what might be said generally about a collection of artists and their work, in relation to their historical and social context. Hence the reference to the Russian European School in the early period, the American early modern dancers and the Central European dancers. In total these would seem to be the major contributors to the emergence of a British school of dance, both classical and modern. The 'Western theatre dance' orientation has narrowed further here to Britain, for a variety of good reasons, not least the immediacy of the situation and an interest in our own cultural heritage, whilst acknowledging that much of the increasing dance interest derives from other countries.

Examples of dances which illustrate the second objective are selected to pinpoint significant developments within classical ballet and modern dance. They allow a distinction to be made, for example, between early and later classical ballet. The emphasis is on characterisations which are broader in scope than in pursuing objective 1. In some senses the kind of approach involved in objective 2 is more easily followed than that of objective 1, but the danger is the temptation to use secondary sources, some of which are of dubious reliability and, because of the width of the topic, of making superficial generalisations. The reference to specific dance works, although not as detailed in the structural sense as in objective 1, is intended as a check against this. By making constant reference back to the actual dances, some depth of study may be achieved. At deeper levels of study the analysis of interacting strands of culture with the production of a particular dance could make a rewarding topic.

Objectives 1 and 2 clarify in different ways two possible approaches to historical study of dance. They are not mutually exclusive; the use of either would be valid. Using both at different times would in total provide a rounded and wide-ranging study area while allowing for analysis in depth of the historical development of certain examples of theatre dance.

Teaching methods
The methods that might be used in teaching the unit are those applicable to any study of dance, i.e. through performance, through lectures, discussions, reading and study of particular written passages; through viewing the dances and analysing them. In the detailed diagrammatic representation which follows (pp. 190–1), the order of types of study method under the heading 'methodology/ resources' is different for each objective. In using the first objective the focus is on forms of dance, hence the dances themselves would have priority. The study of live performances thus comes first in the methodology. The reverse is true for the second objective where the emphasis is on cultural forces which gave rise to the dance. Hence the first category under methodology is the study of contextual writings.

Evaluation
Evaluation is spelled out in terms of the kind of result that would

184

demonstrate whether or not a student had in fact reached some understanding of the historical situation of dance. *What* is evaluated or assessed relates back to the objectives and the content. In this case it is understanding, revealed in the ability to be articulate about selected forms of dance and their historical growth through time, and to attribute these factors to appropriate influences.

It is relevant to both methodology and evaluation that while the more usual form of accounting for historical knowledge is by means of written or verbal statements, practical demonstration of competence might also play a part. Particular help with the written form is given in Chapter 11 'How to structure and write a historical dance study or project'.

10.2 *A foundation unit in dance history*

The foundation unit entitled 'A historical and cultural perspective of twentieth century Western theatre dance' appears in a normal format on page 186. A diagrammatic representation of the same unit is given on pages 190–1 and shows the relationship between aim, objectives, content, methodology and evaluation. The reasons for the selection of material, its organisation, presentation and assessment have been stated earlier in this chapter and there is no necessity for further comment except to draw attention to the specific works to be studied in respect of the first objective. As stated on page 182 these works were selected partly on practical grounds, i.e. their accessibility in company repertoires, on film or through writings. In practice a further criterion for selection, however, would be the teacher's knowledge and choice. As such, the teacher might well decide that works other than those suggested here would be equally appropriate for study if resources are readily available locally. It must be recognised that it is through the study of specific works that the student comes to know about the development through time of selected forms of theatre dance.

The factors that are relevant in determining a course of study are outlined earlier in this chapter. These same factors have to be considered again in selecting *routes* from within the totality of this unit. A major consideration is the amount of time available for study. In addition, students' age, their experience of dance and dance history, approach to study, capacity for written or practical work have to be taken into account. However, these do not so much affect the route followed as the way in which the content of that route is presented.

*FOUNDATION COURSE – A HISTORICAL AND CULTURAL
PERSPECTIVE OF TWENTIETH-
CENTURY WESTERN THEATRE
DANCE*

Aim

An understanding of the historical and cultural context of twentieth century Western theatre dance.

Objectives

1. Consideration of the development through time of selected forms of theatre dance
    a) classical ballet
    b) modern dance
2. Knowledge of examples of different forms of dance which emerged as a result of cultural forces (e.g. artistic, political and social) in Western Europe and the U.S.A.

Content

1. Study of specific manifestations of dance
    a) classical ballet
        i)   From the repertoire of the Diaghilev Ballet in London 1911–29
        ii)   From the Early British period 1930–45
        iii) From the repertoire of the Sadler's Wells/Royal Ballet 1946–63
        iv)   From the Ashton repertoire after the mid 1960s
        v)   From the MacMillan repertoire after the mid 1960s
    b) modern dance
        i)   An early British work 1910–33
        ii)   From the repertoire of the Ballet Jooss in Britain 1933–53
        iii) From the repertoire of Graham's early British seasons – 1954, 1963, 1967
        iv)   From the repertoire of the Ballet Rambert after 1966
        v)   From the repertoire of the London Contemporary Dance Theatre after 1967
2. A study of schools of dance arising from diverse cultures
    a) Russian European School 1905–29
        i   Political and social conditions
        ii) Artistic movements centred on Paris
        As exemplified in the works of Fokine, Nijinsky, promoted by Diaghilev

b) The American School 1897–1905
    i)   Religious and social conditions
    ii) Romantic naturalism
    iii) Expressionism
    As exemplified in the works of Fuller, Duncan, St Denis, Shawn
c) The Central European School 1910–32
    i)   Political and social conditions
    ii) *Ausdruckstanz* – dance of expression
    As exemplified in the works of Laban, Wigman, Jooss
d) The British School 1905–80
    i)   Early classical ballet 1926–66 arising from the Diaghilev influence and the Russian classics.
         Exemplified in the works of de Valois, Ashton, Petipa
    ii) Later classical ballet 1966 onwards, American influences on modern ballets
         Exemplified in the works of MacMillan, Tudor, Tetley
    iii) Early modern dance 1905–66 arising from the Duncan influence.
         Exemplified in the works of Morris, Ginner, Atkinson
    iv) Later modern dance 1966 onwards, arising from the American influence of Graham.
         Exemplified in the works of Bruce, Cohan, Davies, Morrice, North

Methodology
Study of live performances/video/films; dance and music scores; dance criticism; contextual writings of an artistic, social or political nature through lectures, discussions; watching dances; reading and analysing written material; performing extracts.

Evaluation
Through presentation of
    a) a descriptive written account of dances and cultural factors affecting dance
    b) an analysis of similarities and differences between works and schools and through time
    c) an indentification of important factors giving rise to an interpretation

    d)   a written evaluation of overall significance of dances and schools of dance for the historical development of dance.

10.3 *Possible routes for study*

The possibilities for breaking down the unit into smaller and perhaps more manageable parts for study seem vast. Obviously some kind of selection is necessary. The resulting four models are the outcome of such selection, progressive models indicating increasingly specific areas of work. These are as follows:

Model 1 a) Study of the development of selected dance forms through time

           b) Study of the cultural forces affecting dance forms

Model 2 Study of a specific dance form in its historical and cultural context

Model 3 a) Study of a specific dance form through time (represented in the upper half of the diagram)

           b) Study of a specific cultural influence and its effect on selected British dance forms (represented in the lower half of the diagram)

Model 4 Study of a specific dance form in a specific/limited period of time

Model 1

The most obvious division of material would create two routes, i.e. a) and b). Discussion of the course content earlier in this chapter indicates that the foundation unit consists of two mutually supportive strands of enquiry, one concerning the *development through time of dances* in both classical ballet and modern dance and the second concerning *consideration of the cultural forces* which give rise to similarities or trends, which many choreographers of a particular era share. Whilst these routes are considered mutually supportive, as indicated, it is possible to focus on one or the other or indeed, as in the case of this model, to select *either* one route *or* the other. Dividing the material in such a way means that the objective, content, methodology and evaluation for each route would remain the same as that indicated on pages 190–1.

Model 2

Material may be divided so that a *specific dance form is studied in its historical and cultural context*. The diagram on page 192 illustrates such a route. In this model, the form selected for study is modern dance but a similar route could be planned for classical ballet. In the modern dance route the focus is on developments in Britain. The relevance of this to students of dance in this country is obvious. Modern dance is generally regarded as a twentieth century phenomenon hence the time span of the study is defined within the form identified. Since it might be argued that British modern dance owes its existence to influences from abroad, in particular those from Western Europe and the U.S.A., the cultural context must be specified. The range of methods of teaching and evaluation procedures again are those identified on page 191. The content relates to the title, aim and objectives of the course and all are specified in detail on page 192.

Model 3

The two routes identified within this model indicate how material may be selected to give knowledge, in the first instance, of the *development of a specific form in time* and, in the second instance, of a *specific school*. In the former the dance form selected to exemplify this is classical ballet. From the content illustrated on page 194, it may be seen that the concern is for the development of classical ballet in Britain from 1900 to the present day and the focus is on the emergence of The Royal Ballet. The specific nature of the route means that the focus is likely to be on the *structure* of dances of the selected periods. Through the study of choreography, performance and critical writings, the students' knowledge of such developments through time and of their overall significance in terms of the emergence and progress of The Royal Ballet will be increased. Similar routes are clearly possible in relation to modern dance and to the emergence of other companies both classical and modern. A course with such an emphasis might have special relevance to students undergoing a highly specialist training at one of the major dancing academies.

The second route indicated within this model is equally specific but in a quite different way, since the emphasis is less on actual dance structures and more on the context in which such structures

DANCE HISTORY

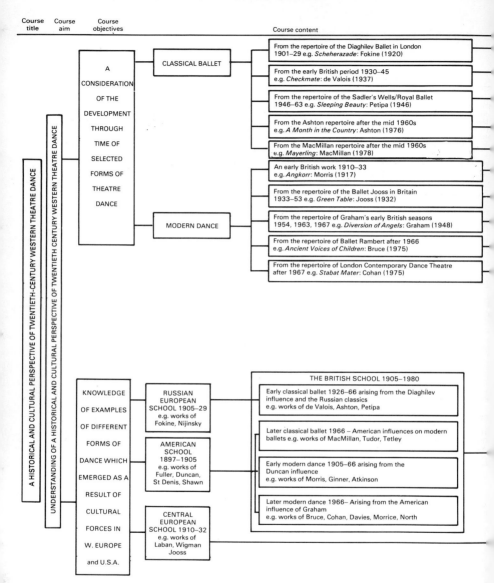

Course title	Course aim	Course objectives		Course content

A HISTORICAL AND CULTURAL PERSPECTIVE OF TWENTIETH-CENTURY WESTERN THEATRE DANCE

UNDERSTANDING OF A HISTORICAL AND CULTURAL PERSPECTIVE OF TWENTIETH CENTURY WESTERN THEATRE DANCE

A CONSIDERATION OF THE DEVELOPMENT THROUGH TIME OF SELECTED FORMS OF THEATRE DANCE

CLASSICAL BALLET

From the repertoire of the Diaghilev Ballet in London 1901–29 e.g. *Scheherazade*: Fokine (1920)

From the early British period 1930–45 e.g. *Checkmate*: de Valois (1937)

From the repertoire of the Sadler's Wells/Royal Ballet 1946–63 e.g. *Sleeping Beauty*: Petipa (1946)

From the Ashton repertoire after the mid 1960s e.g. *A Month in the Country*: Ashton (1976)

From the MacMillan repertoire after the mid 1960s e.g. *Mayerling*: MacMillan (1978)

MODERN DANCE

An early British work 1910–33 e.g. *Angkorr*: Morris (1917)

From the repertoire of the Ballet Jooss in Britain 1933–53 e.g. *Green Table*: Jooss (1932)

From the repertoire of Graham's early British seasons 1954, 1963, 1967 e.g. *Diversion of Angels*: Graham (1948)

From the repertoire of Ballet Rambert after 1966 e.g. *Ancient Voices of Children*: Bruce (1975)

From the repertoire of London Contemporary Dance Theatre after 1967 e.g. *Stabat Mater*: Cohan (1975)

KNOWLEDGE OF EXAMPLES OF DIFFERENT FORMS OF DANCE WHICH EMERGED AS A RESULT OF CULTURAL FORCES IN W. EUROPE and U.S.A.

RUSSIAN EUROPEAN SCHOOL 1905–29 e.g. works of Fokine, Nijinsky

AMERICAN SCHOOL 1897–1905 e.g. works of Fuller, Duncan, St Denis, Shawn

CENTRAL EUROPEAN SCHOOL 1910–32 e.g. works of Laban, Wigman Jooss

THE BRITISH SCHOOL 1905–1980

Early classical ballet 1926–66 arising from the Diaghilev influence and the Russian classics e.g. works of de Valois, Ashton, Petipa

Later classical ballet 1966 – American influences on modern ballets e.g. works of MacMillan, Tudor, Tetley

Early modern dance 1905–66 arising from the Duncan influence e.g. works of Morris, Ginner, Atkinson

Later modern dance 1966– Arising from the American influence of Graham e.g. works of Bruce, Cohan, Davies, Morrice, North

Methodology/resources					Evaluation			
STUDY OF LIVE PERFORM- ANCES	STUDY OF VIDEO/ FILM	STUDY OF SCORES -dance -music	STUDY OF DANCE CRITI- CISMS	STUDY OF OTHER WRITINGS	DESCRIPTIVE WRITTEN ACCOUNT OF WORKS	ANALYSIS OF SIMILARITIES & DIFFERENCES IN WORKS ARISING THROUGH TIME	INTERPR ETATION OF THE SIGNIFICANCE OF DEVELOP- MENTS FOR CLASSICAL BALLET AND MODERN DANCE	EVALUATION OF THE ARTISTIC SIGNIFICANCE OF CHANGES THROUGH TIME

STUDY OF CONTEXTUAL WRITINGS -artistic -social -political	STUDY OF DANCE CRITICISM	STUDY OF SCORES -dance -music	STUDY OF VIDEO/ FILM	STUDY OF LIVE PERFORMANCES	DESCRIPTIVE WRITTEN ACCOUNT OF CULTURAL DIVERSITY AS IT INFLUENCED THE DANCE	ANALYSIS OF THE DIFFERENCES ACROSS CULTURES THROUGH TIME	INTERPRETATION OF SIGNIFICANT FACTORS	EVALUATION OF THE OVERALL SIGNIFICANCE

191

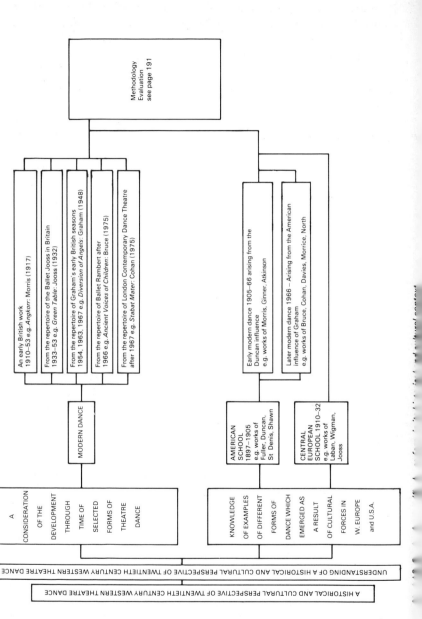

Methodology/Evaluation

Content

Objective

Aim

Title

Methodology
Evaluation
see page 191

MODERN DANCE

An early British work
1910–53 e.g. *Angkorr*: Morris (1917)

From the repertoire of the Ballet Jooss in Britain
1933–53 e.g. *Green Table*: Jooss (1932)

From the repertoire of Graham's early British seasons
1954, 1963, 1967 e.g. *Diversion of Angels*: Graham (1948)

From the repertoire of Ballet Rambert after
1966 e.g. *Ancient Voices of Children*: Bruce (1975)

From the repertoire of London Contemporary Dance Theatre
after 1967 e.g. *Stabat Mater*: Cohan (1975)

A CONSIDERATION OF THE DEVELOPMENT THROUGH TIME OF SELECTED FORMS OF THEATRE DANCE

AMERICAN SCHOOL 1897–1905 e.g. works of Fuller, Duncan, St Denis, Shawn

Early modern dance 1905–66 arising from the Duncan influence
e.g. works of Morris, Ginner, Atkinson

Later modern dance 1966 – Arising from the American influence of Graham
e.g. works of Bruce, Cohan, Davies, Morrice, North

CENTRAL EUROPEAN SCHOOL 1910–32 e.g. works of Laban, Wigman, Jooss

KNOWLEDGE OF EXAMPLES OF DIFFERENT FORMS OF DANCE WHICH EMERGED AS A RESULT OF CULTURAL FORCES IN W. EUROPE and U.S.A.

UNDERSTANDING OF A HISTORICAL AND CULTURAL PERSPECTIVE OF TWENTIETH CENTURY WESTERN THEATRE DANCE

A HISTORICAL AND CULTURAL PERSPECTIVE OF TWENTIETH CENTURY WESTERN THEATRE DANCE

192

have arisen. The example identified is concerned with study of the Central European School 1910–32. Here the focus is on the *social, historical and artistic conditions surrounding groups of artists.* The artists identified are Laban, Wigman and Jooss. Clearly this study area is not as immediately relevant to the students' experience of living dance and this, together with the problems of study in this area identified in Chapter 8, might make it more relevant for study at degree level. Parallel routes might be planned by selecting material appropriately for the Russian European School 1905–29 or the American School 1897–1905.

In respect of each of the routes identified in this model the methodology and assessment procedures identified on page 191 remain the same but differ in their specific requirements. The titles, aims and objectives change and the content is selected accordingly. These details are illustrated in the diagram on pages 194–5.

Model 4

Model 4 identifies a route which not only *limits the particular dance form for study* but also *identifies a very short time span.* This is exemplified using modern dance, as influenced by Martha Graham and realised in Britain, most specifically through the repertoire of London Contemporary Dance Theatre although also to a lesser extent in the repertoire of Ballet Rambert. The selection of content is self-explanatory and appears on page 196. Clearly, in order to determine any influences the study needs to pinpoint the features of Graham's technique and choreography made explicit in her dances and to explore the extent to which such features may or may not be seen in works of other choreographers in London Contemporary Dance Theatre or Ballet Rambert. In this pathway comparison of dances choreographed by Graham, Cohan and Bruce might be approached through an examination of, for example, theme, style, movement vocabulary or formal structures. Methodology and assessment procedures involved are drawn from those identified in the initial diagram on page 191 since the approach for study focuses on both the *structure of the dances* and on the *cultural conditions* which gave rise to them. The title, aims and objectives make explicit the specific nature of the course content and are indicated on page 196.

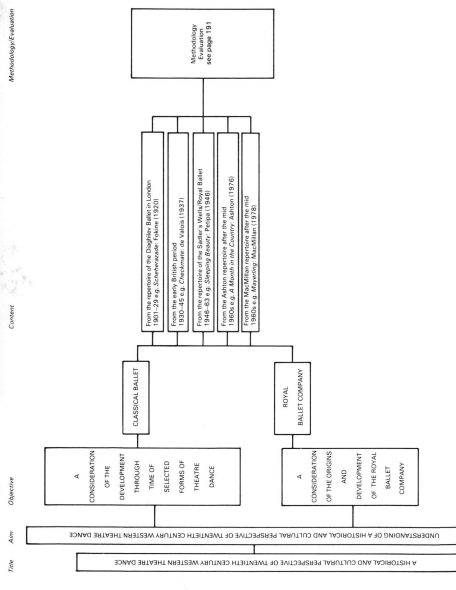

Title · Aim · Objective · Content · Methodology/Evaluation

A HISTORICAL AND CULTURAL PERSPECTIVE OF TWENTIETH CENTURY WESTERN THEATRE DANCE

UNDERSTANDING OF A HISTORICAL AND CULTURAL PERSPECTIVE OF TWENTIETH CENTURY WESTERN THEATRE DANCE

A CONSIDERATION OF THE DEVELOPMENT THROUGH TIME OF SELECTED FORMS OF THEATRE DANCE

A CONSIDERATION OF THE ORIGINS AND DEVELOPMENT OF THE ROYAL BALLET COMPANY

CLASSICAL BALLET

ROYAL BALLET COMPANY

From the repertoire of the Diaghilev Ballet in London 1901–29 e.g. *Scheherazade*: Fokine (1920)

From the early British period 1930–45 e.g. *Checkmate*: de Valois (1937)

From the repertoire of the Sadler's Wells/Royal Ballet 1946–63 e.g. *Sleeping Beauty*: Petipa (1946)

From the Ashton repertoire after the mid 1960s e.g. *A Month in the Country*: Ashton (1976)

From the MacMillan repertoire after the mid 1960s e.g. *Mayerling*: MacMillan (1978)

Methodology Evaluation see page 191

194

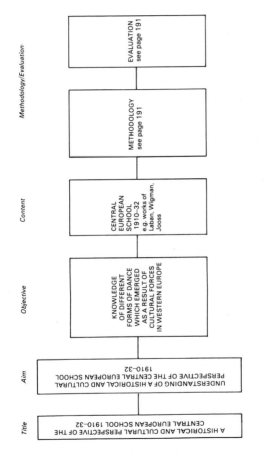

Model 3b: Study of a specific cultural influence and its effect on selected British dance forms

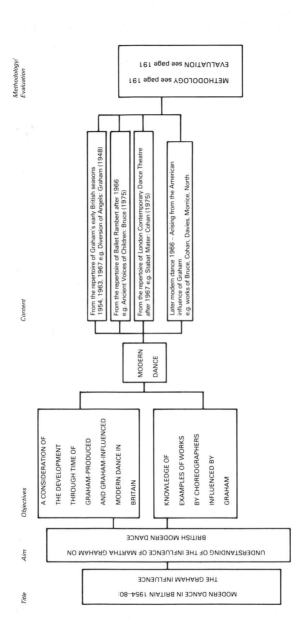

Model 4: A study of a specific dance form in a specific period of time

Further possibilities

The preceding models all arise from the selection of material initially identified in the proposed foundation unit. The suggested pathways focus on study areas which are increasingly specific according to how the material is selected and related. There is no limit to how detailed a study area might become, and the final two examples discussed give some indication of how such specific areas might be studied. In both the focus is on a *particular choreographer*, but whereas in the first example the concern is for the *development of the works of the choreographer through time*, in the second example the *works are examined in the light of their artistic context*. Obviously such an exercise could be carried out in respect of any major artist associated with dance, e.g. performer, composer, designer.

To illustrate the two study routes identified within the overall framework, two choreographers, Ashton and Morrice, are taken as examples. In the case of the former the aim of the course would be to understand the development of Ashton's choreography through a period of time. To realise the aims the student would need to consider specific dances, and the works selected for study would be those deemed significant in Ashton's career as a choreographer. Works might be categorised historically, grouped within periods and certain dances highlighted for study. For example, Ashton's early association with Rambert resulting in his first ballet *A Tragedy of Fashion*, his first choreography after becoming a permanent member of the Vic–Wells Ballet; his first full-length ballet and later works which reflect more lyrical or dramatic emphases, such as *Symphonic Variations* and *Marguerite and Armand* would all provide interesting material. The purpose in selecting dances for study in such a course is that they pinpoint developments in Ashton's choreographic career.

In the second route identified within this model, the course would be equally specific but the focus quite different, the emphasis being on the context. To avoid the danger of a heavy or total dependence on secondary source material, the course could be planned to identify significant works which would reflect the context. The aim of such a course might be to understand artistic influences which have affected the choreographic career of Morrice. However, in order to appreciate such influences, the student would also study Morrice's dances. The content, the dances chosen for study, would need to give rise to the possibility of illustrating different artistic

197

influences. Morrice is a particularly useful example for studies of this kind since in his career he has choreographed dances in both the classical ballet and modern dance styles.

It is immediately obvious that detailed studies of the kind exemplified above may well become highly analytic. Although they could form the basis of a taught course, they might more appropriately be the topic of a dance history study of the kind outlined in Chapter 11.

Summary

Constructing dance history courses requires that an educational rationale and methodology be applied to the specific content of dance history. The creation of small units of study which are complete in their own right is one way of formulating a course, although it is also possible to proceed simply from very general aims. However, the majority of dance teachers have, as yet, very little historical background, hence the attempt here to present clear alternative strategies. The focus throughout is on the dance itself and how that dictates the content of teaching and the methods of procedure. Four models are presented, which concentrate in turn on the dance works produced and on the cultural forces affecting their development. Further possibilities are then outlined.

These frameworks are examples of ways of structuring the vast area of dance history into manageable units of study. The curriculum methods described can be applied to any era in the history of dance.

CHAPTER 11

How to structure and write a historical dance study or project

by Judith A. Chapman

11.1 Structuring a project
11.2 Sources of information
11.3 Analysis and interpretation of source materials
11.4 Historical writing
11.5 A suggested format for the presentation of a historical study
11.6 Guidelines for evaluating a study/project in the history of dance

Probably the most difficult problem to be solved in undertaking a historical investigation is how to define precisely the area for study. The identification of a general topic of interest is obviously a starting point, then begins the process of peeling away layer after layer, selecting and discarding until a clearly defined and manageable problem is focused upon. For example, an initial idea for a project might be to examine the reaction of audiences in this country to performances by American modern dance companies. Through a gradual process of tracing source materials and teasing out ideas such a project, at undergraduate level, might eventually focus on audience reaction in Great Britain to two visits to this country by the Martha Graham Company in 1954 and 1963. Thus, the location, the company and specific dates of performances are defined. In addition, it may be necessary to select and use only a limited range of source materials such as *The Times* or *The Telegraph* newspapers. Within a clear framework for study it is then possible to attempt a thorough analysis of the different sources as they might relate to the topic.

11.1 *Structuring a project*

There are many different ways of categorising types of investigation and the following is offered as an example:

—investigations in relation to individual artists and groups of artists, e.g. choreographers, dancers, companies
—investigations in relation to dances, e.g. types of styles of dance and their performance
—investigations in relation to dance criticism, e.g. critics and audiences
—investigations which are thematic, e.g. use of Greek myths in choreography, theories of dance technique

In any of the above four categories the focus for study may be, and generally must be, further defined by reference to *time*, e.g. 1965–69, or *place*, e.g. in London, or *source materials*, e.g. from writings in the *Dancing Times* or from the writings of a critic such as John Percival.

Of first importance in structuring an area for study is the identification of a clear question or problem and its parameters. This is a process involving general reading and searching out of relevant information in order to generate ideas relating to the topic. Initially such ideas may simply help the student to define more precisely the focus of the study in the kind of framework referred to above, e.g. in time or place, or both. This early stage in setting up a project should also enable the student to identify aspects of the topic which are to be of particular importance, e.g. in studying the work of a choreographer it may be that her/his collaborations with specific dancers or musicians are especially worthy of investigation.

The result of this initial stage should be a more sharply focused question or problem with related subsidiary questions. There needs to be ongoing discussion between student and teacher as source materials are found and as the various facets of the study unfold. An obvious danger is that the multitude of ideas generated may cause confusion about the purpose of the study – i.e. this stage engenders a greater complexity and, seemingly, a larger area for study than originally envisaged. However, it is as a result of this that the student, with guidance from the teacher, will be better able to analyse the facts and the explanations that might possibly be related to a problem and then be in a position to proceed to explore thoroughly the relationships between these factors.

During this initial stage modifications will be made to what was originally conceived as the topic for study. This may lead to a narrowing of the topic along the lines outlined previously or to a reslanting of the main question as a result of new information.

For any student whose knowledge of the history of dance is of a rather general kind this stage of becoming aware of different facets of a possible topic is an extremely important one and the time required may be considerable. However, a precise focus with a possible structure for developing and presenting ideas needs to be identified in order that work can proceed within a clear framework, though it must be remembered that the finding of additional source materials may, of necessity, lead to changes in the structure of the project.

11.2 *Sources of information*

Having clearly identified the focus of the question or problem for study and its parameters, it is necessary to identify and collate all available source materials. A general principle of procedure is from secondary to primary source materials (for definition see Chapter 2). Dance dictionaries or encyclopedias (see Appendix A) may be used initially to provide background information. Details are, of necessity, brief but a lead is established for further investigation. Secondary sources are used when primary sources are not available and also as a means of tracing other primary sources. Secondary source materials are, in this sense, a starting point for study. They are (as already outlined in Chapter 2) an interpretation of primary source materials, or even of other secondary sources, and thus will provide a particular author's views and bias. In this latter sense they are of use in comparing and contrasting different interpretations of a particular event or of the same primary source material. Previous studies may be tapped for relevant methodology and concepts in addition to evaluating the validity of their interpretations and conclusions. Having identified and collated all available source materials it is necessary then to select from them in relation to the focus of the study and parameters already clarified. Information used should be relevant to the stated problem.

11.3 *Analysis and interpretation of source materials*

Analysis of information collated should bring together pertinent data and theories, weaving them into a network of relationships that highlights relevant issues, revealing gaps in knowledge and preparing the way for the logical step to hypothesis construction. In the analysis and interpretation of source materials it is necessary to show an understanding of the contemporary situation, i.e. the context of the time at which the material was written. One purpose in a historical project might be to raise questions about possible relations between such factors as social organisations, religion, and the arts. In order to appreciate any development in dance generally or a particular dance work, it is necessary to understand something of its historical context. This is not to deny that some really important things about dance or dance works may have very little to do with historical context; what is being said is that appreciation of dance or of a particular dance work may be added to by an understanding of the historical context. Furthermore, it should be realised that connections between historical context and developments in any art are complex and the best kind of historical investigation will explore and analyse the infinitely subtle relations between social and historical factors and particular works of art.

Historians, like scientists, do disagree with one another, and it must be accepted that all historical writing is ultimately interpretation. However, this does not mean that 'one opinion is as good as another'.

> Imagination, the ability to penetrate beyond the facts to the connections between them, is expected but in a history essay you must be guided first of all by the information you have acquired from your various sources. There is all the difference in the world between creative historical imagination and sheer invention (that is, in this connection, simply making things up).
>
> (Open University, Unit 8, 1970, p. 22)

Historical controversy is of value and contributes towards historical truth if it leads to the critical testing of a particular hypothesis or generalisation and/or leads to a new line of enquiry.

Recently acquired source materials may lead to reconsideration of the overall structure of the investigation as already stated. Alternatively, additional source material may lead to questions being generated with regard to some fact/event/interpretation that previously had been accepted. This stage of the process of historical investigation may best be likened to detective work where a new piece of evidence casts existing theories in doubt or at least leads to them being examined from a different perspective. Reference has

202

been made for the most part in this section to written source materials. It is acknowledged that visual and audio source materials offer distinct possibilities but they also present problems for analysis and interpretation (see Chapter 2). They are mentioned here since their usefulness in enhancing and supplementing written sources of information must not be overlooked.

The actual existence of either primary or secondary historical sources does not guarantee their authenticity, accuracy or validity. The student of history must be constantly critical of the materials obtained. Sources must always be evaluated with an understanding of the times and conditions under which they were produced, for example customs and codes of conduct change with time and, therefore, the student needs to be familiar with the prevailing culture within which the historical events being examined occurred. The following points on evaluation might be used for reference:

1. Concern with authenticity:
   —who is the author?
   —what are the qualifications of the author?
   —is the author well informed?

2. Concern with meaning and accuracy:
   —do the words mean the same now as then?
   —is the author biased?
   —are the facts presented by a document in accordance with other known facts?
   —how soon after the event was the document written?

The sources from which information is obtained should always be clearly identified. Wherever there is a direct quotation there should be a reference to author, the date of publication and a page reference. Wherever a particular point or idea has been derived from a source, this source should be identified. This applies equally to the summarising and/or paraphrasing of the words of another writer. The appropriation of the writings or ideas of another in order to pass them off as one's own is known as 'plagiarism'. This literary 'theft' is no more acceptable than theft of any other kind. It is important not to overdo the use of direct quotation. 'Scissors-and-paste' is the term sometimes applied to a piece of historical writing which looks as though the writer has simply cut up chunks of other people's work and pasted them together.

11.4 *Historical writing*

The structure for presenting the study/project will need to be decided in relation to the topic investigated and the source materials available to the student.

The following points may be helpful:

Introduction

Brief explanation of the context of the study/project e.g. identifying the period/location of the study; general historical, social, artistic context to be examined; why the topic is of sufficient significance to provide the focus for a study; main body of source materials which are used.

Review of relevant literature

This will need to be sub-divided into, for example, secondary/primary source materials, periods of time, distinct aspects of the topic.

Analysis and interpretation of source materials cited

Ideas contained within source materials will need to be teased out and implications identified and made explicit; comparison of source materials in order to identify controversy and conflict; analysis of historical context; reference will need to be made to authenticity, reliability and value (see Chapter 2).

Discussion of wider implications

Analysis and interpretation of source materials will lead to a consideration of these findings in relation to an understanding of dance history and an attempt to place the study in context.

Conclusions

Conclusions must be logically and adequately argued and clearly dependent on material presented in the earlier sections of the study/project. Major conclusions should be presented first. Reference should be made to the problem identified for study in the introduction.

Suggestions for further study

It may be possible to indicate briefly where gaps in knowledge exist or to identify what may be worthwhile pathways for future investigations.

References and/or bibliography
The former should list only those references included in the main text of the study, but a bibliography consists of all the works consulted whether or not they are specifically referred to. There are various acceptable formats for presenting references and bibliographies; the one essential rule is that all such material must be cited in full and in a consistent manner so that readers can follow up any individual item.

11.5 *A suggested format for the presentation of a historical study*
    Title page
    Abstract
    Table of contents
    Introduction
    Review of relevant literature
    Analysis and interpretation of source materials cited
    Discussion of wider implications
    Conclusions
    Suggestions for further study
    Appendix/appendices
    References and/or bibliography

11.6 *Guidelines for evaluating a study/project in the history of dance*
In writing up a study/project the following checklist may be of use:

11.6.1 *Title of the investigation*
    Does the title clearly identify the area of the problem?
    Is the title concise, precise and descriptive?
    Are superfluous words and vague or misleading phrases avoided?

11.6.2 *Description and statement of the problem*
    Has a thorough analysis been made of all the facts and the explanations that might be related to a problem?
    Are arguments and explanations logically sound?
    Does the statement of the problem appear early in the study?
    Is it clearly identified?

11.6.3 *Scope of the problem*

Is the problem sufficiently delimited to permit an exhaustive treatment, e.g. in time: 1910–15; during the nineteenth century.

e.g. sources: as evidenced by the writing of the time; from the writing of Clive Barnes

e.g. location: in America; in Bath

e.g. in scope: in the theatre; in education.

11.6.4. *Presentation, analysis and interpretation of source materials*

Has efficient and critical use been made of all available source materials?

Is all information relevant to the stated problem?

Is information communicated in a clear and precise manner?

Does the study achieve a reasonable balance between description, analysis and interpretation?

Are source materials evaluated appropriately?

Does the review of literature, the analysis and interpretation of source materials collated merely present facts and leave the reader to assimilate the ideas and draw conclusions concerning their relationship to the study/project? *Or* does the writer bring together pertinent facts and theories and weave them into a network of relationships that points out relevant issues, reveals gaps in knowledge and lays a foundation for logical deductions and insights?

Is the study/project successful in investigating not merely what happened but why and under what circumstances?

Does the interpretation of source materials show understanding of the contemporary situation?

Is documentation accurate and the bibliography complete?

In suggesting approaches to the structuring and writing of a historical study or project, it is difficult to encapsulate the very real excitement that can result from involvement in a historical investigation of the kind outlined in this book. Perhaps the analogy with detective work used earlier can serve to illustrate the stages of searching out information, the piecing together and comparing of different accounts, the sifting of evidence in order to tease out fact from fiction. There is a satisfaction which comes from having searched for and eventually found a piece of information which has perhaps shed new light on some previously unremarked event. The jigsaw puzzle, if not complete, reveals a little more of its picture!

Reference

Open University 1970 *Common pitfalls in historical writing*. Humanities Foundation Course A100, Unit 8

Appendix A

Basic reference texts

1. *Bibliographies*

Beaumont, C. W. 1929, 1963 *A bibliography of dancing.* New York: Blom

Beaumont, C. W. (ed.) 1966 *A bibliography of the dance collection of Doris Niles and Serge Leslie,* part I A–K. London: Beaumont

Beaumont, C. W. (ed.) 1968 *A bibliography of the dance collection of Doris Niles and Serge Leslie,* part II L–Z. London: Beaumont

Beaumont, C. W. (ed.) 1974 *A bibliography of the dance collection of Doris Niles and Serge Leslie,* part III A–Z. Mainly twentieth century publications. London: Beaumont

Davis, M. 1972 *Understanding body movement. An annotated bibliography.* New York: Arno Press

Derra de Moroda, F. 1982 *The dance library.* Munich: Wolfie

Fletcher, I. F. 1977 *Bibliographical descriptions of forty rare books relating to the art of dancing in the collection of P. J. S. Richardson.* London: Dance Books

Forrester, F. S. 1968 *Ballet in England: a bibliography and survey c. 1700–June 1966.* London: Library Association

Leslie, S. (ann.) 1981 *A bibliography of the dance collection of Doris Niles and Serge Leslie,* part IV A–Z. Mainly twentieth century publications. London: Dance Books

Magriel, P. 1936, 1966 *A bibliography of dancing. A list of books and articles on the dance and related subjects.* New York: Blom

2. *Dictionaries*

Gadan, F. & Maillard, R. 1959 *A dictionary of modern ballet.* London: Methuen

Koegler, H. 1982 *Concise Oxford dictionary of ballet.* London: O.U.P.

New York Public Library 1974 *Dictionary catalogue of the dance collection* (10 vols.). Boston: G. K. Hall

New York Public Library 1975, 1976, 1977, 1978, 1979, 1980, 1981,
1982 *Supplements to the dictionary catalogue of the dance collection*
Raffé, W. G. & Purden, M. E. (comp.' & ed.) 1964. *Dictionary of the
Dance* London: Yoseloff
Wilson, G. B. L. 1974, *A dictionary of ballet* (3rd ed.). London: A. C.
Black

3. Encyclopedias

Chujoy, A. & Manchester, P. W. (eds.) 1967 *The dance encyclopedia.*
New York: Simon and Schuster
Clarke, M. & Vaughan, D. (eds.) 1977 *The encyclopedia of dance and
ballet.* London: Pitman

4. Guides

Belknap, S. Y. 1959–63 *Guide to dance periodicals*, vols 1–10. New
York: The Scarecrow Press
Brinson, P. & Crisp, C. 1970 *Ballet for all. A guide to one hundred ballets.*
London: Pan Books
Brinson, P. & Crisp, C. 1980 *Ballet and dance: a guide to the repertory.*
London: David & Charles
Clarke, M. & Crisp, C. 1981 *The ballet-goer's guide.* London: Michael
Joseph
McDonagh, D. 1976 *Complete guide to modern dance.* New York:
Doubleday

5. Journals/Periodicals (past and current)

Ballet 1939, 1946–7, then *Ballet and Opera* 1948–49, *Ballet* 1950–52
Ballet Annual 1947–64
Ballet Review (U.S.A.) 1965–
CORD: – Dance Research Journal 1974–
    CORD News 1967–74
Dance and Dancers 1950–June 1980, September 1981–
Dance Chronicle (U.S.A.) 1976–
Dance Index 1942–48
Dance Magazine 1925–
Dance Perspectives 1959–75

Dance Research (U.K.) 1983–
Dance Scope 1965–82
Dance Studies (Centre for Dance Studies, Jersey) 1976–
Dancing Times (1894–1909), 1910–
Folk Music Journal 1965–
Journal of the English Folk Dance and Song Society 1936–
Laban Art of Movement Guild Magazine 1947, from 1982 *Movement and Dance, Magazine of the Laban Guild*
New Dance 1977–
2D (Dance and Drama) 1981–

6. *Research Listings*

American Alliance (formerly Association) for Health, Physical Education and Recreation. National Section on Dance. In Esther E. Pease (ed.) *Compilation of Dance Research 1901–1964.* Washington D.C.: A.A.H.P.E.R., 1964
Dance Division. *Research in Dance I.* Washington D.C.: A.A.H.P.E.R., 1968
Dance Division. *Research in Dance II* Washington D.C.: A.A.H.P.E.R., 1973
Dance Division. *Research in Dance III* Washington D.C: A.A.H.P.E.R. 1982
See also research listings under Dissertation Abstracts.

Appendix B

The National Resource Centre for Dance, University of Surrey

1. *Introduction*

The setting up of a National Resource Centre for Dance (N.R.C.D.) was a key recommendation in the report of the Calouste Gulbenkian Foundation enquiry into 'Dance education and training in Britain' (1980, p. 182). The N.R.C.D. was established on the University of Surrey campus in October 1981 with an initial grant from the Calouste Gulbenkian Foundation. At the same time the Foundation also funded the establishment of an academic department of Dance Studies at the University of Surrey to develop undergraduate and postgraduate degrees and research work in dance. June Layson took up the joint post of Director of Dance Studies and Director of the N.R.C.D. in October 1981 and was joined in January 1982 by Judith Chapman as Research Officer for the N.R.C.D.

The N.R.C.D. functions as a separate institution closely inter-related with the overall academic development of dance at the University of Surrey and will eventually be self-financing. The Gulbenkian initiative in promoting dance through both academic study and resource management has been welcomed wholeheartedly by all sectors of the dance profession.

2. *The N.R.C.D. brief*

The Resource Centre is committed to making information about dance easily accessible. All types of dance are encompassed with a particular emphasis on dance in the U.K. The N.R.C.D. brief is

—to provide information on dance to individuals, institutions, dance companies, organisations and societies from its own computerised data base and also by identifying and locating materials held elsewhere;

—to establish a dance archive consisting of notated, sound, visual and written materials particularly emphasising the dance of the U.K.;

—to prepare and produce teaching and learning materials for dance together with dance publications on a variety of topics.

Interpretation of the brief

2.1 *The N.R.C.D. and information access*

There is no doubt that many resources for dance exist but they are scattered throughout the U.K. and sometimes uncatalogued. The task of locating all individual dance items is a daunting one but work is in progress to locate and analyse substantial holdings of materials on dance in the U.K. Information about holdings is being collated and will be computerised so that it is retrievable in a variety of ways to meet consumer needs and interests. The N.R.C.D. will act, therefore, as an information centre and as a national co-ordinating agent and access point.

The N.R.C.D. will eventually provide a service whereby an individual can obtain a computer print-out listing sources on a particular dance topic. The information storage and retrieval system will also facilitate the publication of a regular current awareness bulletin and of bibliographies on selected topics.

2.2 *The N.R.C.D. as a dance archive*

The Dance Collection of the New York Public Library has become a repository for all kinds of information about dance and, similarly, it is planned that the N.R.C.D. will become a national dance archive in the U.K. It is envisaged that the N.R.C.D. will complement the work of existing organisations such as the English Folk Dance and Song Society and the Theatre Museum which already have specific archival functions. The initial stages in the establishment of the dance archive can only be achieved through the vision and generosity of people who donate materials and funds or who are willing to place their dance collections in the archives of the N.R.C.D. It is encouraging that some individuals, societies and companies have already donated materials to the N.R.C.D. and discussions are taking place with others who wish to deposit or loan their collections.

The N.R.C.D. has initiated a programme to make visual and

audio recordings and, thereby, to generate its own archive materials. Plans have been made to produce video recordings of current dances and these, together with notated scores and other written records, will be preserved for future generations. In addition, audio recordings in the form of interviews and general reminiscences will provide an unparalleled source of information about dance. Key figures in the dance world will be encouraged to talk, to discuss and to record for posterity their particular perception of the dance of their time.

2.3 The N.R.C.D. and the publication of dance materials

Market research is being carried out in order to explore consumers' needs and to identify priorities amongst the many types of topics and formats which could be prepared. Visual, written, notated and sound materials will be produced as separate items and in combination in response to stated needs. Initially publications will be basic listings such as bibliographies, choreochronicles and fact sheets.

In 1982 the N.R.C.D. produced the first of its basic information-giving publications. This is a *Dance Film and Video* catalogue of currently available material which will be updated periodically and eventually be fully annotated.

3. Timing of developments

The location of existing resources for dance in the U.K. and the development of a computerised information storage and retrieval system which will facilitate access to those materials are priority tasks. It is anticipated that the structures for achieving this will be clarified during 1983 and it is anticipated that work will begin on computerisation during 1984. The locating of materials, classifying and storing of information is a continuous process and the dance data base will be updated as previously unknown resources are discovered or become available.

It is planned that in the long-term public access to the N.R.C.D. will be by telephone, post, on-line computer terminals and/or visits. Of these four access modes one, i.e. by post, is currently operative. This means that items of information can be ordered and purchased by post through individual and institutional subscription rates.

4. The physical location of the N.R.C.D.

The N.R.C.D. is currently housed in offices next to the Dance

Studies department of the University of Surrey. The University is to launch a public appeal for the building of a Performing Arts Centre on the campus. This centre will have a theatre, accommodation for the academic Dance Studies department and the University's well established Music department, and include purpose-built accommodation for the N.R.C.D. The public part of the N.R.C.D. building will have an open exhibition area and be equipped with computer terminals, facilities for viewing film and video in addition to a large study space with controlled access to special collections and archives. The other main areas of the N.R.C.D. will contain the cataloguing rooms, notation preparation rooms, air-conditioned and temperature controlled archival storage rooms as well as staff and technicians' offices.

The N.R.C.D. accommodation will link with the Dance Studies building so that one of the many dance studios will be available for N.R.C.D. purposes such as notation, reconstruction and video-recording.

5. *The N.R.C.D. and the student of dance history*

Although it will be several years before the N.R.C.D. is fully operational and housed in purpose-built facilities, it is evident that it is already beginning to meet many of the needs of those interested in dance information and resources. When the N.R.C.D.'s services are increased and it fulfils its brief of developing a computerised dance data base, establishing a dance archive and producing dance materials, full international computer links will be established with similar centres and organisations. The national and potential international role of the N.R.C.D. make it a valuable institution for those interested in the study of dance history.

INDEX

Many dancers, choreographers and theorists are cited within the text. The index includes only those whose works are described at some length.

INDEX

216